# The Intelligent Curriculum

# The Intelligent Curriculum

Using MI to Develop Your
Students' Full Potential

DAVID LAZEAR

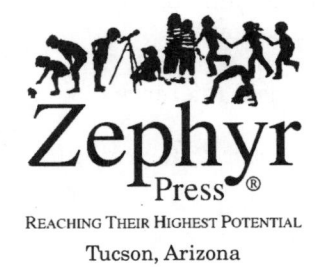

Zephyr
Press ®

REACHING THEIR HIGHEST POTENTIAL
Tucson, Arizona

The Intelligent Curriculum
Using MI to Develop Your Students' Full Potential

Grades: K through 12

© 2000 by Zephyr Press
Printed in the United States of America

ISBN 1-56976-099-3

Editing: Veronica Durie and Stacey Shropshire
Cover design: Daniel Miedaner
Design and production: Daniel Miedaner
Illustrations: Shaun Bailey

Zephyr Press
P.O. Box 66006
Tucson, AZ 85728-6006
1-800-232-2187
http://www.zephyrpress.com

Library of Congress Cataloging-in-Publication Data
Lazear, David G.
      The intelligent curriculum : using MI to develop your students'
full potential / David Lazear.
          p.     cm.
      Includes bibliographical references (p.  ).
      ISBN 1-56976-099-3
      1. Multiple intelligences.  2. Learning.  3. Curriculum planning.
      I. Title.
      LB1060.L385   1999                                      99-34599
      375'.001—dc21

*With its expanded image of what it means to be human, the theory of multiple intelligences underscores the responsibility of educational institutions to engage each child's talents. Somewhere in his or her schooling career, it is vital that each child discover at least one area of strength. The student may then delight in pursuing an area of inherent skill and intrinsic interest. Such pursuits not only nurture joy in learning, but also they fuel the required persistence and effort necessary for mastery and inventiveness. Conversely, if students do not discover an area or areas of interest, they may never develop an interest in learning and may instead travel aimlessly through school or abandon formal learning altogether.*

—Linda Campbell, Bruce Campbell, and Dee Dickinson
*Teaching and Learning through Multiple Intelligences*

# Contents

# Foreword

It is clear that David Lazear believes in people. From reading this book (and his other works), one cannot help but come away with a feeling of optimism and hope for the future. He understands that the theory of multiple intelligences (MI) is a tool, a way of looking at students and of developing curriculum and assessment tools that increases the likelihood that students will learn. He understands teachers' needs and offers ways for them to bring the intelligences into their classrooms each day.

In *The Intelligent Curriculum,* David shares several approaches to pursuing MI: a Year-Long Curriculum Journey, Unit Stretching, MI Stations or Centers, and a Schoolwide Focus. The approaches vary in their scope and ambition but share a hands-on approach to MI. Taken together, they offer much to the teacher who is just learning about MI and much to the veteran MI practitioner. Teachers (and administrators) who use this book will find themselves stretched and engaged in new activities, and in new ways to look at kids.

The book is filled with practical ideas and hands-on strategies for bringing MI to life. For example, in the section on the Year-Long Curriculum Journey, tables show the intersection of the various intelligences, something that stirs creative juices and offers some specific directions. Teachers who use this book will have a better idea *how* to use the various intelligences in the classrooms to increase student success. Similarly pragmatic, both the Learning Center and Unit Stretching models enable teachers to build from their current curriculum, to use MI in ways that enhance curriculum, instruction, and assessment. Throughout the book, David lists the positive and negative aspects of the various approaches, helping readers view and consider the various strategies within their unique contexts.

I am most taken by the section on the Schoolwide Focus. Roland Barth's notion of "collegiality" is implicit here, and the positive result is a setting in which students and teachers learn and grow together. As we have learned from more than a decade of implementing MI at the New City School, the key to faculty success is learning together (and making mistakes together) as colleagues. Granted, not every teacher is fortunate enough to work in a building in which MI can be embraced and pursued by all. Even for those who work in isolation, however, this model can serve as an inspiration and a goal.

The last section of the book, which addresses teaching *about, with, through,* and *for* multiple intelligences, is thought provoking. There is much fodder here for school decision makers, from teacher leaders to principals to central office administrators to school board members! David recognizes that "parent education"— indeed, "community education"—is an ongoing process. Not unlike the painting of the Golden Gate Bridge, one is never finished.

Thomas R. Hoerr, Ph.D.
New City School
St. Louis, Mo.
May 1999

# Preface

At this writing I have been consciously working with the theory of multiple intelligences for almost a decade, and unconsciously for much longer, without having a name for what I was exploring. During this past decade I have been impressed by some of the impacts the theory of multiple intelligence is having in the educational realm. Much is changing as people become aware of MI and the immense difference it can make in students' schooling and in their lives beyond school. Although none of these trends have reached their full maturity, and this list is not exhaustive, some that are most exciting to me and those that inspire hope in me follow:

## Instructional Practice

In countless situations I have witnessed, often firsthand, a dramatic transformation of teachers' instructional practice as I get the opportunity to observe and work with them in their classrooms. Other times I hear about the transformation via stories they tell in workshops. As teachers start to implement MI, their teaching becomes much more multimodal and they design lessons to address all the unique learning needs of all students by using all of the intelligences. Students are deeply and thoughtfully involved with the material and thus learn and understand it much more thoroughly on more levels of their brain, mind, body systems.

## Curriculum Balance

Changes are happening in the curriculum as people become more and more aware of its verbal-linguistic and logical-mathematical biases. We are beginning to value the development of students' full range of intellectual and cognitive abilities, not just "reading, writing, and 'rithmetic." In fact, the curriculum integration models I present in this book have all been adapted from schools, districts, and school divisions involved in curriculum restructuring from an MI perspective.

## Students' Understanding (and Expecting!) of MI

More and more, as teachers start teaching *with* multiple intelligences, they find it necessary to teach their students *about* multiple intelligences, as well. In most cases they don't so much add on to content as they simply add a layer of metacognitive awareness that students can bring to bear on the learning process, regardless of the content.

## Moving beyond Labeling of Students

More and more I see teachers and administrators struggling to get away from the old practice of labeling students as LD, gifted, special education, and so on, to a practice of trying to understand the unique intellectual profiles of their students: "What makes this kid tick intellectually?" And what is even more heartening is they are using the information presciptively, to help more students be successful in school

## Parent Inservices

Many districts and school divisions have started to take the inservicing of parents as seriously as they do the inservicing of their professional teaching staff. The most effective of these inservices not only informs parents about MI in the school, but also gives them ideas of things they can do at home to appreciate and nurture the full spectrum of their children's intelligences.

## Assessment

When MI theory enters the school *and* is seriously implemented in the teaching process, it causes a profound crisis in assessment practices and assumptions. However, this crisis is good. We are seeing and understanding more deeply all the time the unfairness of teaching using all eight intelligences, then assessing students' understanding using only two. In fact, to assess students using only verbal-linguistic and logical-mathematical intelligences does not give us a true picture of what students have in fact learned in the classroom. Slowly, slowly, but surely, surely, tests and testing practices are changing and becoming more authentic and more in line with the different ways of knowing.

Now, I am not naive. Multiple intelligence theory is not a panacea; it will not cure every ill we are facing in our schools, nor solve every problem. But it does bring some very significant pieces to the school restructuring conversation. In its conception, MI was not an educational theory at all. It was a theory much more related to human development and to what it is to live a full life, "cooking on all eight (and maybe more) of your burners!" For far too many years we have made the learner fit the school. In some ways I like to say that MI is humanizing school so that it fits the learner.

At the same time so much good is happening, the cry from the public, from school board officials, and legislators (elected by that public!) is "Back to basics!" Yet when one asks what these "basics" are that we should get back to, often the real answer, underneath the platitudes about the importance of literacy and the importance of math skills for getting a job, is "Students must be able to memorize various bodies of information, which someone, at some time in the past, decided should be the focus of a formal education, then be able to spit this information back out in different forms on various standardized tests." When students are successful at memorizing and regurgitating, we say, "Ah, they're really doing well in school. They're getting a good education." When they are not successful, we go after the schools and say, "Teachers just aren't doing their jobs! Our schools are going down the tubes!"

If I had the financial resources, organizational skills, and political clout, I would love to set up a series of town meetings across the United States and Canada to address some basic questions to help us define the basics:

- What is the end product, so to speak, we want out of our schools?

- What in fact is our definition of an educated person, and how would we know if and when education is successfully going on?

■ What are the key life and work skills people will need to live successful, happy, productive lives in the twenty-first century?

■ What is the "core knowledge" that all students should master and deeply understand? Why do we feel it is core knowledge?

This book is my attempt to give my tentative answers to the first three of these questions. It is a book about *curriculum integration using the multiple intelligences as the integrating factor*; it is not about what the content of the curriculum should be. It is rather concerned to show how, in and through *whatever* the content is, we can help students develop their full intellectual potential! It is my deep belief that by working with our students to help them activate and use the various capacities of the eight intelligences, we are in fact setting them on a pathway of reaching their full potential as human beings. I can think of no greater gift that one can give another person than this.

Special thanks goes to several schools and districts that were the inspiration for the four approaches to integrating the curriculum with MI you will encounter in the pages that follow:

■ The El Paso Independent School District in El Paso, Texas, invited me to work for three weeks with their curriculum task force, and that is where the Year-Long Curriculum Journey model was hammered out.

■ The Mount Pleasant Catholic Education Center in Cleveland, Ohio, and the Elk Elementary Center in Charleston, West Virginia, gave me the idea for the Schoolwide Focus model.

■ Robert Kapheim, a retired science teacher from York High School in Elmhurst, Illinois, helped me conceive the Unit Stretching model as he talked to me often about how he taught various units in his classroom.

■ The truly inspired work of Bruce Campbell—an elementary teacher in the Marysville School District in Washington State, a wonderful national presenter on the topic of implementing multiple intelligences in the classroom, and an author—taught me about the MI Stations and Learning Centers model.

There are countless others—personal acquaintances, family, friends, and most especially, my partner Jim Reedy—whom I must thank for their continued support, encouragement, prodding, patience, and sometimes cajoling that must occur whenever I find myself in the midst of writing another book.

David G. Lazear
Maui, Hawai'i
1999

# 1

# The Case for Integrating MI into the Curriculum

*P*aul is a three-year-old and will be entering preschool soon. He is very excited about going to school and can't wait for the day to arrive. He feels good about himself and the many things he can do. He loves to sing and make music with "instruments" of his own creation. The walls of his room at home are filled with drawings, paintings, and simple montages he has created. He loves to sculpt things from clay. Paul has many friends in the neighborhood. The parents of these children enable them to get together frequently.

*Paul enters preschool and goes on to kindergarten where every day is filled with new explorations and new learning. Learning is fun! It is an adventure! He learns through play, through interaction with the other children, through movement, through music and dance, and through art and creating things with his hands. He has frequent contact with the natural world, sometimes by going outdoors, other times by bringing nature in: animals, plants, rocks, leaves, interesting sticks or logs, bugs, and so on.*

*The room is open so there is plenty of space to move around. It is filled with toys, games, books, colors, and textures. There are several computers loaded with software containing early childhood learning games and activities. Music is frequently playing in the room. The teacher often sings instructions related to tasks the children are to perform, such as cleaning up the room or going to the potty. She also sings about curricular concepts being taught and learned. The children participate in lots of pretending, imagining they are animals or characters in stories the teacher reads to them. They learn dances from other lands. Every day they participate in many activities that utilize the full range of the senses. Every day they have time alone for silent reflection.*

*Throughout the day, Paul has the opportunity to continue what he began as an infant—the opportunity to live at least part of the time as a self-directed learner. He has the opportunity to make choices critical to his becoming what we most want children to become—a lifelong learner.*

*Paul loves school. He is sad at the end of the day. He can't wait for the next day to come so he can return to this environment. On weekends he goes through withdrawal.*

Ask yourself this question: *How long do you suppose Paul's positive experience with school will last? How long do you think he will continue to look forward to being there?*

Imagine yourself walking into almost any preschool or kindergarten class in almost any nation of our world. Ask the children, "How many of you know how to sing?" "How many of you are good drawers?" "How many here can dance?" "Who really likes working with and playing with other people?" How many hands do you think will go up? It is my experience that, in every case, almost every hand will go up.

Now try the same set of questions in a typical third-grade class: "How many of you can sing?" "Who can draw?" "Who likes to dance?" and so on. Usually only one-third to one-half of the hands will go up. Often as early as grade three the "I can'ts" have set in.

Try asking the same set of questions of a typical group of middle school students. How many hands will go up? Probably three or four, but even these students will raise their hands hesitatingly, as if they were embarrassed, for they are worried about what their peers will think.

Finally, try these questions in the typical high school classroom. You may find yourself asking "Does anyone here even know how to raise his or her hand?" No hands will go up! Usually by the middle and high school years, most of the things that made school so exciting and meaningful in the early years, things that were fun, engaging, exciting, provocative, and evocative, are treated as "optional," as "*extra*curricular." They are included only when (and if) there's time. They have, for all practical purposes, been moved to the far edges of the curriculum as the governing attitude is "It's time to end play and get down to the serious work of getting an education."

Ever since I started working with the theory of multiple intelligences, I have felt that if people want to see what a *natural learner* looks like, they should look at children when they first show up on the doorsteps of our preschools. Generally, the students are all bubbling away like little pots on a stove, with the savory stew of their intelligences inside. What usually happens as students proceed through their formal schooling is that year by year by year, we take some ingredients out of that pot, put the lid on this pot, turn down the heat over here, even remove some of the pots from the stove altogether. Children start to hate school. They start to feel bad about themselves and their capacities as human beings. Many feel stupid. They develop negative feelings about one another—especially those who don't fit the mold of what school is "supposed to be" all about. Check it out in your district or school; how early do the "I can'ts" start? How early do children start saying "I'm not very good at X"? By the time they reach middle and high school, a large number of students are just putting in the time the law requires. And of course, many will drop out of school at the first available legal opportunity.

## Keeping the Intelligences Alive

This book addresses the questions:

- ■ What if we could keep alive throughout students' schooling what is alive in them when they first come to us?

- ■ What if there were a way to maintain the love and adventure of learning through grade 12 and beyond?

- ■ What if we could conduct formal schooling in such a way that intelligence shutdown, and the concomitant learning shutdown, didn't happen?

- ■ What if year by year, instead of doing less and less with the various intelligences, we did more and more?

- ■ What if the curriculum were spiraled in such a way that the early experience of learning were extended across the entire educational journey in ways that are *developmentally appropriate*?

I believe that by working with a multiple intelligences approach to integrating the curriculum, we can indeed keep the intelligences alive in students K–12 and beyond, and thus reverse the process I have described above.

## Curricular Content and the Intelligences

It is important to point out that integrating MI into the curriculum is not a matter of changing content. In fact, many people often make this mistake when they begin working with the multiple intelligences; that is, they equate certain content areas with intelligence counterparts. For example, they tie the visual-spatial intelligence to the art curriculum, the bodily-kinesthetic intelligence to PE, the auditory-vibrational intelligence to various music curricula, and so on. In a recent article for *Phi Delta Kappan,* Howard Gardner states that we should not confuse an intelligence with a particular domain or discipline, or in the case of this book, a given curricular area:

> An *intelligence* is a biological and psychological potential; that potential is capable of being realized to a greater or lesser extent as a consequence of the experiential, cultural, and motivational factors that affect a person . . . In contrast, a domain [discipline, curricular area] is an organized set of activities within a culture . . . in which individuals participate on more than a casual basis, and in which degrees of expertise can be identified and nurtured . . . Thus physics, chess, gardening, and rap music are all domains in Western culture. Any domain can be realized through the use of several intelligences. (202)

If there are curricular content implications of the theory of multiple intelligences, I believe the best approach would be a course of study on multiple intelligences itself, which would give students an opportunity to get to know themselves intellectually. It would involve a study of each of the intelligences and their related capacities, research and projects that would help students understand their own intellectual profiles, ways to enhance and develop their less-developed intelligences, and ways to use the various intelligences to effectively meet the challenges of daily living or to help with problem solving on the job, in one's family, or in one's personal life. There are some beginning suggestions for what might be included in this MI curriculum in my book *Pathways of Learning: Teaching Students and Parents about Multiple Intelligences.* Such a course is not necessary, however, to incorporate the intelligences into the existing curriculum.

While equating the various intelligences with various curricular areas is not harmful to students, from a philosophical and cognitive perspective it avoids the real issue of **systematically helping students develop their full intellectual potential in, through, and across the curriculum.** A stronger way to make my point is that it is a copout to say, for example, "Well, the art teacher is dealing with their visual-spatial intelligence and the PE teacher is hitting their bodily-kinesthetic intelligence; I don't have to worry about those two intelligences in my classroom or in my content area." Then we are missing the point. Would we think it acceptable to say the same about the development of their verbal-linguistic intelligence? We realize it makes no sense whatsoever to say, "The language arts teacher is dealing with their verbal-linguistic intelligence, so I don't need to worry about understanding what my students are saying, how well they are spelling, or how effectively they are communicating." In most schools, districts, or school divisions, such a statement would be considered to be just this side of heresy! However, we don't even bat an eye when teachers have this attitude about the other intelligences.

This book advocates a variety of curriculum integration approaches that suggest that, regardless of content area, we all must become the art teachers, the PE teachers, the music teachers in and through whatever content we are teaching! I'm not suggesting that we usurp the critical roles of the art, music, drama, PE, and dance instructors, nor teach the unique content of these disciplines. These curricular areas are very important in their own right, and they need to be an integral part of every student's educational journey. In other words, music as a content area is important for its own sake, whether or not it can be used in math, science, language arts, and so on. The same can be said about all of the so-called fine arts parts of the curriculum. Why not simply call all parts of the curriculum the academic areas? What makes math, science, history, language arts, and so on more academic than drama, dance, PE, art, music, and so on? One of the greatest travesties that exists in public education in both the United States and Canada (and in many other nations as well!) is that the fine arts programs are often the first to be cut when school districts or divisions run into financial difficulties. I believe that they are the last programs that should be cut, for, to whatever degree the intelligences are still alive in our students, it is these programs we have to thank! Now, again, while there is not a direct correlation between the intelligences and these content areas, they nevertheless have had a part in "nurturing the intelligences." I am suggesting that, regardless of what the content is, we can incorporate the capacities of the intelligences into the teaching and learning process, thus providing students with a more holistic educational experience that gives them the chance to develop their full intellectual potential and capabilities in and through their mastery of the curriculum.

In this book, my focus is on helping our students fully develop all their intelligences. When we help them develop to their full potential, we offer them the most important gift we can, for we set them up for their future life more effectively than we could simply with any curricular content. Please do not misconstrue what I am saying; I am very concerned about the mastery of certain core concepts necessary for students to be successful in our postmodern world. I am attempting to put the curriculum in perspective: Content is relative and changing, whereas the intelligences are ontological; that is, they are innate, bioneurological, cognitive potentials that in many ways define our unique being as humans. Students need all of the intelligences to understand, utilize, and master the new information and skills they will need in the new millennium.

## Integrating MI into the Curriculum: Why Is It Important?

This book presents four models for embedding various capacities of the intelligences into whatever content your curriculum addresses. In other words, as students go through the curriculum, they have multiple opportunities to utilize their multiple intelligences in the very act of dealing with, understanding, learning, processing, and acquiring the knowledge present in the curriculum.

When one decides to broach the topic of curriculum integration, one has entered a complex, diverse, and controversial realm of dialogue—a realm full of creative challenges that must be faced, conundrums which must be solved, and many mine fields that must be avoided!  Chapman (1993) sums up one of the major issues: "Some compare the school curricula to a sausage that everyone and anyone can stuff with anything they desire (including state bird day, state flower day, and the life cycle of the cockroach). This leaves teachers to wait for the overstuffed curriculum to explode or to find meaningful ways to abandon the trivial" (199).

In *Multiple Intelligences: The Theory in Practice,* Howard Gardner makes the following observation regarding the deeper issue of the "overstuffed" curriculum:

> **If one wishes to have any chance of securing understanding, it becomes essential to abandon the misguided effort to "cover everything." Broad coverage ensures superficiality: at best, heads become stuffed with facts that are forgotten almost as soon as the short answer test has been administered. Rather, one must move toward "uncoverage," or, to cite another current slogan, one must embrace the principle that "less is more" . . .**

> **It is important to define at the outset the kinds of concepts that one wishes students to understand and the kinds of performances that one wishes students to exhibit upon the completion of school. Once defined, these "end states" or "final exhibitions" become the basis on which curricula and assessments to be used en route are then devised. (191)**

Part of the good news about this book is that a multiple intelligence approach to integrating the curriculum is not a matter of curriculum "add ons"! I am not suggesting more "stuff"! Rather, I am suggesting that in and through whatever the "stuff" of the curriculum is, integrating multiple intelligences will help you help students to develop the full range of their potential intelligences, thereby ensuring a deeper, more thorough and authentic understanding of that "stuff."

Nor am I suggesting that the major movements for curriculum reform and restructuring that are occurring in most nations of our world are unimportant. Quite the contrary; they are extremely important, especially when we consider the knowledge base people will require to live effectively in the new century! However, the so-called new curricular content must move far beyond what was required in the past. We are currently living in a global society that is multicultural beyond our wildest imaginings. The technological advances boggle the mind, with what qualifies as state-of-the-art seeming to change on an almost daily basis. What some have called "our shrinking world" becomes more and more a daily reality; due to technology, one can shop in Paris, chat with someone in Chile, and get a picture of a favorite celebrity without ever having to leave the chair in front of the computer. In addition, one can have breakfast at home in New York, have a business luncheon meeting in Paris, and be back home for dinner with his or her family in the evening!

Although the content of the curriculum is not the primary concern of this book, I would like to share Gardner's comments regarding curricular reform and reevaluation:

> I favor some forms of "core knowledge," some materials that all students should know. Note that this preference does not take the form of a canonical list of books or principles: I do not feel that such a mandate is appropriate or well founded. Rather, I search for a consensus around certain very rich or generative concepts, like evolution or democracy; and for attention to the kinds of performances that can reveal understanding, such as the application of those concepts to newly encountered biological phenomena or political occurrences. (Gardner 1991, 192)

I feel that building the consensus that Gardner suggests here should be at the heart of any curriculum adoption discussions. Rather than teaching a curriculum per se, we should be focusing on fully developing profound understanding of the core knowledge and the "performances that can reveal understanding" on which we have agreed. The curriculum is but a resource to be used in the development of these rich, generative themes. Curriculum is often a very good resource, I must point out, but a resource nonetheless—it's not holy writ! Part of the problem with any prepackaged curriculum is that, along with it, you must also buy the biases of its creators. In *Teaching and Learning through Multiple Intelligences,* the authors make the following important observation which any educators should bear in mind when looking to adopt a new curriculum:

Over the years, numerous curriculum trends have proliferated, each with its own philosophic assumptions, goals, and teaching and learning processes. With the advent of Gardner's theory, educators are now able to scrutinize any curricular model through [eight] lenses to see if it includes the full range of human capacities. When one does so, it becomes readily apparent that many programs actually have a strong bias. They appear to be founded on one or two intelligences while excluding the others. (Campbell et al. 1992, 190)

When educators and the larger community discuss such things as core knowledge, foundational skills, values, and so on, which we believe are desired outcomes of the formal educational journey, they become empowered to create their own curricula based on their discussion. It is only after this discussion, which one hopes would lead to consensus, that we should consider various curriculum packages and printed, audio, and video materials. Even then, the materials must serve only as hand-maidens, so to speak, to the pursuit of these common educational goals. Howard Gardner (1991) makes the following comment on this topic:

> Far too much of what is taught today is included primarily for historical reasons. Even teachers, not to mention students, often cannot explain why a certain topic needs to be covered in school. We need to reconfigure curricula so that they focus on skills, knowledge, and above all, understandings that are truly desirable in our country today, and we need to adapt those curricula as much as possible to the particular learning styles and strengths of students. (79)

And so, what is curriculum integration? There are as many definitions of curriculum integration as people you ask. Also, within the realm of curriculum integration there are many levels and degrees of integration that are being implemented within schools, districts, and school divisions.

In this book, when I talk about curriculum integration, I am talking about *embedding the capacities of the various intelligences into the existing curriculum* or weaving them into the curriculum in such a fashion that students have the opportunity, in and through their study of the required curriculum, to develop, enhance, strengthen, and amplify their many intelligences.

## What's in the Book and How to Get the Most out of It

In the following pages, you will find a description of the various capacities of the various intelligences (chapter 2) and four practical models for integrating MI into the curriculum; here the integrating factor is the multiple intelligences (chapters 3 through 6). In each chapter that deals with a model, you will find a concrete example of what the model might look like applied to typical elementary, middle school, and high school curriculum material. The presentation of each model includes a discussion of special considerations given the unique nature of dealing with students at these various developmental levels.

In all of my work with the theory of multiple intelligences, whether it be professional development workshops and training seminars, or the written, audio, and video resources I have produced, my passion and firm commitment are to provide highly practical approaches to implementing MI in school districts or school divisions, individual schools, and individual classrooms. You will find that my commitment to this goal runs throughout this book, as well.

Please note that nothing I have presented will work as is. You've got to work with each integration model to make it your own. I hope my role is one of a catalyst to get your own creative juices flowing! The following suggestions for using the book come from the assumption that, to deeply understand this approach to MI integration, you must work with the processes I have presented and make sense of them in the particulars of your own professional context:

**Step 1**    **Understand the purpose of each of the curriculum integration models.** Study the descriptions I provide at the beginning of each chapter; they provide important background information, philosophical presuppositions, and implementation guidelines. Focus on the intent of the approach suggested rather than the particulars of implementation.

**Step 2**    **Study the three examples for each model.** They are intended to demonstrate ways to use the model with typical curricular content at the elementary, middle school, and high school levels. Regardless of your teaching level, I suggest you digest each example to help you discover both the possibilities and limits of each approach. Then focus on the particulars of implementation, always thinking about your teaching situation, regardless of which level of example you are studying.

**Step 3**    **Examine the pluses and minuses for each model.** I suggest that you create your own lists. *On the positive side*, list what you really like about each of the models I've presented: Where do you see instant applications? What about a given model makes the most sense to you? How will it help you incorporate more of the intelligences into your instruction and into students' learning? *On the negative side*, list what you don't like about each model: What parts of it just aren't practical in the "real teaching world"? Where do you find yourself saying, "Good idea, but I'm not sure how it could be implemented in my situation"? What just doesn't appeal to you about a given model (for whatever reason)?

**Step 4** **Once you feel comfortable with and understand the models, take some of your own curricular material through each one.** In each chapter you will find a step-by-step process for implementing each model. Work your way systematically through these steps. Use the work sheets I provide. Doing this step will help you move from an academic evaluation of my examples to testing their possibilities (and limits!) with your own curricular material.

**Step 5** **Take time to do the adaptation reflection log for each model.** In my opinion, these are the most important pages in the book. They are designed to intensify and deepen your experience with the examples by using the specifics of your curriculum. In terms of Bloom's now-famous taxonomy, this step is the higher-order processing part of working with this material. It is the metacognitive aspect. The reason I feel it is the most important part is that, as you engage in this kind of dialogue to process and reflect on what I've suggested, transfer, synthesis, integration, and creative leaps in the possibilities of application can occur—leaps that I hope will take you way beyond any of my ideas and suggestions.

I must also make a disclaimer regarding the examples presented in these chapters. I am not, in the first instance, making suggestions about what the content of the curriculum should be, nor about things that should be added to the existing curriculum. Does the content of the curriculum need to be reevaluated? Yes, it probably does, given that, at the present writing, we are a matter of months away from the turn of the century! However, content is not the concern of this book. What I am concerned with is the notion that, whatever the "stuff" of the curriculum is, in and through that stuff we can use MI to help students develop more and more of their full intellectual potential.

# 2

# MI Capacities

*The Key to Integrating
MI into the Curriculum*

*Possibly genetic factors set some kind of upper bound on the extent to which an intelligence may be realized or modified in the course of a human life. As a practical matter, however, it is likely to be the case that this biological limit is rarely if ever approached. Given enough exposure to the materials of an intelligence, nearly anyone who is not brain damaged can achieve quite significant results in that intellectual realm . . . By the same token, no one—whatever his or her biological potential—is likely to develop an intelligence without at least some opportunities for exploration of the materials that elicit a particular intellectual strength.*

—Howard Gardner
*Frames of Mind* (47)

This chapter is about understanding the core capacities for each of the eight intelligences. In some ways, using the intelligences is like any skill we develop in our lives—the more you use them, practice them, or exercise them, the better and stronger they become in your life, and the more comfortable you will be working within their unique realms.

Let's begin this chapter with the key question I posed in the previous chapter, for it is the focus question for everything that follows: "What if we could keep alive in students throughout their schooling what is alive in them when they first come to us?" I believe we can keep them alive as learners if we seriously seek to understand the individual capacities of the various intelligences.

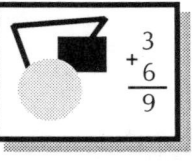

## Logical-Mathematical Intelligence

The knowing that occurs through the process of seeking and discovering patterns and through problem solving. It uses such tools as calculation, thinking skills, numbers, scientific reasoning, logic, abstract symbols, and pattern recognition.

## Verbal-Linguistic Intelligence

The knowing that occurs through the written, spoken, and read aspects of language as a formal system. It uses such tools as essays, debates, public speech, poetry, formal and informal conversation, creative writing, and linguistic-based humor (riddles, puns, jokes).

## Visual-Spatial Intelligence

The knowing that occurs through seeing both externally (with the physical eyes) and internally (with the mind's eye). It uses such tools as drawing, painting, sculpture, collage, montage, visualization, imagination, pretending, and creating mental images.

## Intrapersonal Intelligence

The knowing that occurs through introspection, metacognition (thinking about thinking), self-reflection, and "cosmic questioning" (What is the meaning of life?). It uses such tools as affective processing, journals, thinking logs, teaching for transfer, higher-order thinking, and self-esteem practices.

# *8 Ways of Knowing**

## Musical-Rhythmic Intelligence

The knowing that occurs through hearing, sound, vibrational patterns, rhythm, and tonal patterns, including the full range of potential sounds produced with the vocal chords. It utilizes such tools as singing, musical instruments, environmental sounds, tonal associations, and the endless rhythmic possibilities of life.

## Interpersonal Intelligence

The knowing that occurs through person-to-person relating, communication, teamwork, and collaboration. It employs such tools as cooperative learning, empathy, social skills, team competitions, and group projects that foster positive interdependence.

## Naturalist Intelligence

The knowing that occurs through encounters with the natural world that involve appreciation for and understanding of the various flora and fauna, recognition of species membership, and the ability to relate to living organisms. It uses such tools as hands-on labs, field trips, sensory stimulation, and attempts to classify and comprehend natural patterns.

## Bodily-Kinesthetic Intelligence

The knowing that occurs through physical movement and performance (learning by doing). It employs such tools as dance, drama, physical games, mime, role-play, body language, physical exercise, and inventing.

*Adapted from *Eight Ways of Knowing: Teaching for Multiple Intelligences* by David Lazear (Palatine, Ill.: Skylight, 1998).

As I also mentioned in the last chapter, the key to keeping the intelligences alive in our students, or to preventing intelligence shut down, is to embed the various capacities in the existing curriculum so that, in and through whatever the content of the curriculum is, you are helping students develop their full intellectual potential. In the introductory quotation, Howard Gardner (1983) says it much better than I: "Given enough exposure to the materials of an intelligence, nearly anyone . . . can achieve quite significant results in that intellectual realm" (47). Integrating the curriculum with MI is simply a matter of providing students with a plethora of opportunities for "exploration of the materials that elicit a particular intellectual strength" *in and through their study of the curriculum*!

In Howard Gardner's original research (1983), one of the qualifying criteria for an intelligence was a clearly identifiable set of "core operations" within the brain, mind, body system: "Central to my notion of an intelligence is the existence of *one or more* basic information processes, operations, or mechanisms, which can deal with specific kinds of input. One might go so far as to define a human intelligence as a neural mechanism or computational system that is genetically programmed to be activated or 'triggered' by certain kinds of internally or externally presented information" (64). Thus, when embedding the capacities in the curriculum, a particular unit of instruction, or even a specific lesson, you incorporate the appropriate tasks, activities, strategies, tools, exercises, techniques, methods, and so on that trigger, awaken, and stimulate the various intelligences and their respective capacities.

A second criterion that Gardner brings to bear in determining whether an intelligence qualifies as such is a developmental history:

> **An intelligence should have an identifiable history, through which normal as well as gifted individuals pass in the course of ontogeny . . . It should prove possible to identify disparate levels of expertise in the development of an intelligence, ranging from the universal beginnings through which every novice passes to exceedingly high levels of competence, which may be visible only in individuals with unusual talent and/or special training . . . Identification of the developmental history of the intelligence, and analysis of its susceptibility to modification and training, is of the highest import for educational practitioners. (64–65)**

This developmental history involves more than the development of an intelligence from the level of novice to master; when we view it from the findings of developmental psychology, we find evidence that part of an intelligence's development is related to our human development from infancy to adulthood. Elsewhere in Gardner's work, he has analyzed the growth of the intelligences from an evolutionary perspective; namely, looking at the development of the various cognitive capacities of the intelligences within the journey of the human species to the present moment. In two of my books I attempt to provide detailed summaries of the developmental journey of each intelligence. In *Eight Ways of Knowing* and *Multiple Intelligence Approaches to Assessment* I have presented a developmental template that I applied to each intelligence. It moves from the *basic level* (the raw patterning of the intelligence in early childhood) to the *complex level* (the acquisition of a greater repertoire of skills and learning to apply the skills acquired in the early years) to the *higher-order* or *coherence level* (the integration of the intelligence into one's daily repertoire for living) to the *vocational and avocational level* (often visible through certain careers and hobbies where one has attained high levels of mastery in using a given intelligence).

So why is this developmental characteristic important for the task of integrating MI into the curriculum? An awareness of this *developmental trajectory* (as Gardner calls it) helps us work with the various intelligences in ways that are developmentally appropriate for all students. In workshops, I frequently hear the comment, "Multiple intelligences is great for younger children, but it won't work with high school or post-secondary students." This error results from a lack of understanding of the developmental aspects of the intelligences. Our intelligences don't suddenly go away when we reach a certain age. They may enter various states of latency if we neglect them or if we don't continue to use them on a regular basis. In several previous books, I have cited the work of Jerome Bruner, which deals with the "spiral curriculum." Bruner suggests that you can teach *anything* to *any person* at *any age* **if** you crawl inside the worldview of that person at that particular stage of life and speak the language appropriate within that worldview. In working with the various capacities of the intelligences, the same thing applies; that is, you can involve preschool and high school students in working with the same capacities if you "spiral" what you do with the capacities so they are developmentally on target.

You must take care not to take age divisions too seriously. I am making broad brush strokes, so to speak, to illustrate ways an intelligence tends to grow and develop. No template, no matter who develops it, can dictate how an individual should develop. It is critical to remember that each individual is unique and must be treated so.

It is the core operations, which I call "MI capacities," that we seek to embed in the curriculum in the remainder of this book. In the capacity wheels on pages 19 and 20 and in the following pages are descriptions of the various capacities of the intelligences.

## The Object-Based Intelligences

These intelligences are triggered by the concrete shapes, patterns, colors, images, designs, and objects in the external world with which we come into contact and interact daily. These so-called triggering objects include not only the innumerable objects, shapes, patterns, colors, textures, images that we encounter in the world around us but also those objects we see with our mind's eyes, through such things as visualization and imagination. Without these objects to interact with, these intelligences would have nothing to do!

### Visual-Spatial Intelligence

In our society, we often hear the expression "A picture is worth a thousand words." We often use the cliche "Seeing is believing." We have become a people who love the visual media. We rely on television to provide us with everything from the evening news to a vast array of entertainment possibilities, including "live" concerts of our favorite performers, detective shows, situation comedies, soap operas, and travel logs. We have shopping channels that provide us with opportunities to purchase everything from clothes, food, and other daily necessities to a wide variety of "luxury items," including diamond rings, food processors, audiovisual equipment, vacations, computerized lawn mowers, and automobiles. TV ratings confirm that we love opportunities to see our favorite stars and other famous people interviewed on various talk shows and human interest specials.

In many ways, visual-spatial intelligence is the first language of the brain. The brain naturally thinks in images and pictures before it even has words to attach to them. You could no more stop your brain from visualizing than you could your lungs from

*Adapted from David Lazear's *Eight Ways of Knowing: Teaching for Multiple Intelligences* (Arlington Heights, Ill.: Skylight, 1998).

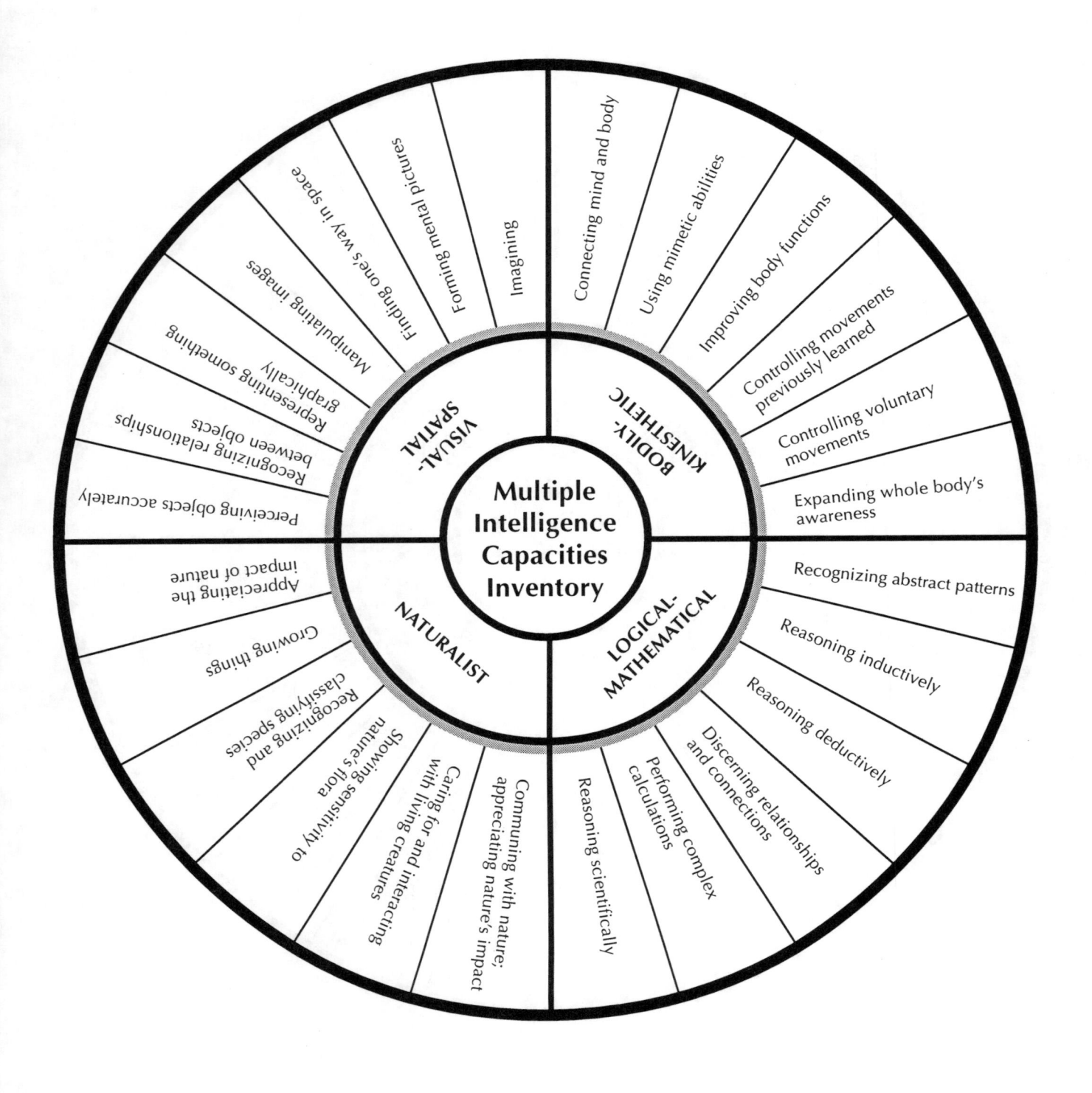

Multiple
Intelligence
Capacities
Inventory

**VISUAL-SPATIAL**
- Imagining
- Forming mental pictures
- Finding one's way in space
- Manipulating images
- Representing something graphically
- Recognizing relationships between objects
- Perceiving objects accurately

**BODILY-KINESTHETIC**
- Connecting mind and body
- Using mimetic abilities
- Improving body functions
- Controlling movements previously learned
- Controlling voluntary movements
- Expanding whole body's awareness

**NATURALIST**
- Appreciating the impact of nature
- Growing things
- Recognizing and classifying species
- Showing sensitivity to nature's flora
- Caring for and interacting with living creatures
- Communing with nature; appreciating nature's impact

**LOGICAL-MATHEMATICAL**
- Recognizing abstract patterns
- Reasoning inductively
- Reasoning deductively
- Discerning relationships and connections
- Performing complex calculations
- Reasoning scientifically

*Adapted from David Lazear's *Eight Ways of Knowing: Teaching for Multiple Intelligences*
(Arlington Heights, Ill.: Skylight, 1998).

taking in oxygen! And yet, often, due to lack of regular exercising and use of these visual-spatial capacities, they are not as strong as they could be.

Part of the task of building the capacities of visual-spatial intelligence is learning to speak the unique language of visual-spatial intelligence; that is, learning to decipher its special jargon, to understand its vernacular, and then being willing to immerse yourself in its various operating modalities. The language and operating modality of visual-spatial intelligence is that of colors, shapes, designs, textures, patterns, images, pictures, and visual symbols.

Let's do a quick inventory of the core capacities of visual-spatial intelligence:

- Remember when you were a kid and you would lie on you back and look up at the clouds and find animals, faces, objects, and different scenes? This capacity is called *active imagination.*

- *Forming mental images* is the capacity to picture things inside your head. You use this capacity when you are trying to remember where you parked your car, where you last used your glasses when you can't find them, or when you are reading a novel and you create mental images of what is on the written page.

- How good are you at following directions for getting from one place to another? Some people are never lost! Others are never found! The capacity for *finding your way in space* is one of the spatial skills of visual-spatial intelligence.

- *Graphic representation* is the capacity to create visual illustrations to enhance communication of an idea, concept, emotion, process, or intuition. This capacity includes such things as photography, sculpture, drawing, painting, videos, and collages.

- Another spatial capacity is *recognizing relationships between objects in space.* How good are you at parallel parking a car? Can you "sink" a basketball into the hoop more times than not? When playing chess or checkers, can you see the whole board and plan your next move in light of this?

■ When you are looking at an "optical illusion" such as the classic two faces that are also a vase, or the old woman who is also a beautiful socialite, can you mentally make these images shift back and forth? Can you see the 3-D images in the various Magic Eye pictures? This capacity is called ***mental manipulation of images.***

■ Have you ever noticed how, if you show very young children an object from several different angles or perspectives, they will sometimes think you have shown them different objects? The capacity of ***accurate perception from various angles*** is the very complex, often taken-for-granted, ability to recognize similarities and differences between objects from very different vantage points.

### Bodily-Kinesthetic Intelligence

For a moment imagine that you are visiting our society from another planet on a typical weekend. You might think you had happened upon a culture obsessed with the skills of the body! You would see stadiums filled with people going wild over various sports competitions. You would find theaters packed with crowds watching live plays and the performances of new dance troupes. In the parks and along almost every roadway, you would see hundreds of joggers, bicyclists, roller bladers, and walkers. If you went to several gyms and fitness centers, you would find hundreds more lifting weights, doing aerobics, exercising on treadmills, and working their way through a variety of complex and strange machines (many of which look like medieval torture instruments). And if you visited a dance club or discotheque, you would find the dance floor jammed with bodies, gyrating and contorting themselves in almost every conceivable position. Educators talk about the importance of "learning by doing." Industry and business are concerned with providing "hands-on" training that ranges from how to work certain machines to how to operate a computer to role-playing new styles of management. One can purchase a mind-boggling array of do-it-yourself videos that demonstrate and lead you through the performance of everything from country western line dancing to gourmet cooking to weight loss to origami and meditation. Some of the highest paid professionals in our society are athletes, actors and actresses, and individuals skilled in the art of dance.

And just consider what you are willing to pay for the services of a plumber, electrician, auto mechanic, or a skilled carpenter—all of which require a high degree of bodily-kinesthetic capability.

Bodily-kinesthetic intelligence may be one of the most taken-for-granted parts of our lives. We perform a wide variety of complex tasks in our daily lives, usually without giving them a second thought. We cross the street and are not struck by on-coming cars. When an object is thrown to us, we instinctively catch it or we duck to avoid being hit by it. Our fingers "know" our telephone number or a computer keyboard. Part of the job of building your bodily-kinesthetic capacities is to practice making the "unconscious" bodily-kinesthetic stuff "conscious." Just consider how often people accidentally hurt themselves simply by being unaware of how the body works, for example, by picking up a heavy object or walking on an icy sidewalk.

The first task in building bodily-kinesthetic capacities is learning to operate within its language system. The language and operating modality of bodily-kinesthetic intelligence is all related to physical movement. This involves such things as drama, mime, dance, gesture, facial expressions, role-play, body language, posture, physical exercise, and physical games.

Let's do a quick inventory of the core capacities that are part of bodily-kinesthetic intelligence:

- Remember when you were a kid and you would practice rubbing your stomach and patting your head at the same time, then switch to rubbing your head and patting your stomach? This skill is sometimes called *multitracking* and is the capacity to learn to **control voluntary body movements.**

- Some of our body movements were at one time carefully and methodically learned and practiced but are today second nature to us, such as walking, riding a bike, driving a car, and so on. Learning to **control these pre-programmed body movements** is one of the capacities of strengthening your bodily-kinesthetic intelligence.

- **Expanding awareness through the body** is the capacity of learning to listen to and trust the body. In many ways the body is like a complex radar station that gives us invaluable feedback about what is happening in the external world; for example, the body shivers in the cold, telling us we need more clothes, or our heartbeat increases and we experience tension in situations of danger.

■ What happens in the mind can profoundly affect the body and vice versa. Think about the effect on your body of vividly imaging your favorite dessert, or imagine the sound of fingernails scraping on a blackboard and notice your physical reaction. This capacity is ***establishing a strong mind-body connection.***

■ How good are you at playing charades? How aware are you of people's body language and their use of physical gestures when they are talking? Such people as Marcel Marsceau and Red Skelton perfected this capacity, called ***mimetic abilities,*** which includes the capacity to mime, to role-play, and to act dramatically.

■ The final bodily-kinesthetic capacity is ***improved body functioning.*** If we direct our awareness to almost any physical activity, we can, through conscious practice, improve our performance, whether it be our serve in tennis, using our nondominant hand, or parallel parking a car. With bodily-kinesthetic intelligence, almost more than any of the other intelligences, practice makes perfect (or at least improvement).

## Naturalist Intelligence

Close your eyes and imagine that you are in your favorite natural setting right now. Imagine that all of your senses are "wide open" and that you can experience the fullness of this setting at 100 percent of what your senses bring in. What are you seeing? What are you hearing and smelling? What textures do you feel? What tastes are in your mouth (or *could be* if you sampled them)? Now move to your "inner senses." What emotions does this place evoke in you? What does it cause you to ponder? What symbols do you see? What is stirred in your soul as you imagine yourself being here?

Welcome to the naturalist intelligence! The naturalist intelligence, the most recent to be identified by Howard Gardner, is directly related to our recognition, appreciation, and understanding of the natural world. You experience this intelligence when you notice the effect on your mood and sense of well-being when someone brings plants or cut flowers into an otherwise sterile, human-created environment. You experience this intelligence when you encounter a newborn animal. Think how often we head for nature when we want to relax, unwind, find inner renewal, or just get away from it all. Consider your reaction to powerful displays of nature's force in such things as the weather or a natural disaster, or the experience of awe evoked by various natural phenomena such as the Grand Canyon, the experience of the changing leaves in eastern Canada or New England, or the ocean's waves ceaselessly crashing on a rock shore. And consider the esteem in which you hold hunters and gatherers and those skilled in herbal medicine, and such figures as John Audubon, Jacques Cousteau, Jane Goodall, Annie Dillard, Beatrix Potter, Tom Woodcock, forest rangers, zookeepers, and so on.

The first task in building the capacities of the naturalist intelligence is learning to operate within its language system. The language and operating modality of the naturalist intelligence is the full sensory impact of the natural world, as opposed to that world created by human beings.

Let's do a quick inventory of the core capacities that are involved in the naturalist intelligence:

- ■ You may know people whom you can take outdoors into almost any natural setting, and they suddenly feel at home. They have developed a special knowing related to the various natural patterns, colors, sounds, smells, textures, shapes, tastes, and so on. This capacity is called ***communion with nature***.

- ■ ***Sensitivity to nature's flora*** involves our relationship to, appreciation of, understanding of, and connection to the plant kingdom. It deals exclusively with the remarkable impact of botanical organisms and the profound knowing about our world and ourselves that can result.

- ■ ***Ability to care for, tame, and interact with living creatures*** is the special skill or talent some have developed for understanding and relating to our fellow creatures beyond the human species. Some people have an almost uncanny relationship with animals—there seems to be an understanding between them.

■ *Appreciating nature's impact* is an attuning of your awareness to the full impact of the environment on you, through, for example, the senses, your emotions, your spiritual awareness, and an awareness of *your* impact on the environment.

■ *Recognizing and classifying species* involves several levels of classification related to animal and plant species of the natural world, including the ability to chart relationships and connections among several species. The skill includes the recognition of membership groups within a species, their unique characteristics, the recognition of neighboring species.

■ *Growing things* involves the nurturing of our special connection to the earth that comes from tilling the soil and living off the land. The knowing here is related to the process of planting something and nurturing it to full growth and maturity.

### Logical-Mathematical Intelligence

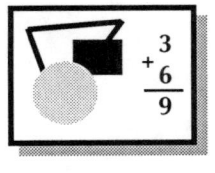

Logical-mathematical intelligence is a pattern-seeking intelligence. When I was in school, if teachers had told me that math is really about patterns, I think I would have done much better in math classes. I thought math was about numbers. I really don't care much for numbers. But I love patterns. Numbers are really only abstract symbols that point to concrete patterns we have seen.

We start doing math (that is, hunting for patterns) very early in our human development. One of the best articulations of what this intelligence is all about is still found in Piaget and Inhelder's (1972) classic work on child development. They trace the various stages in this intelligence's development. The first stage of the development of logical-mathematical intelligence begins with our manipulation of and play with a variety of concrete objects in the physical world around us. It then moves to the recognition of familiar, previously manipulated objects that are placed within a range of other, unfamiliar objects. We develop the capacity to recognize familiar objects in pictures and to pick them out of pictures containing many other objects that are unfamiliar. Eventually, as this intelligence continues to grow, we are able to visualize and imagine these objects when they are not actually physically present. As we acquire language, we also gain abstract verbal symbols that point to the concrete objects we have manipulated.

As logical-mathematical intelligence develops, it gets more and more abstract and symbolic. We see a concrete pattern such as apple, apple, apple, apple, apple, orange, orange, orange. Instead of having to repeat the concrete pattern when talking with another person, we create an abstract symbol called a number to point to the concrete pattern we observe. We talk about 5 apples and 3 oranges. In the concrete everyday world, you will never find the number 5 or 3 apart from its application to a concrete pattern.

In many higher-level math and logic courses in high schools and universities, there is a loss of the concrete world altogether. You have abstractions in thinking about other abstractions and symbolic logic creating symbols for other systems of symbols! You will find numbers existing in their own right as ideal abstractions that need no correspondence in the concrete world to make sense.

Let's do a quick inventory of the core capacities that comprise logical-mathematical intelligence:

- ■ *Abstract pattern recognition* is the capacity to discern patterns in the environment around you. For example, can you find definite repeating patterns in the natural world—spiral patterns, star patterns, triangles, and so on? Can you easily recognize architectural patterns or the pattern scheme someone used in laying the tiles in a bathroom? Are you able to decipher codes and quickly understand symbolic logic?

- ■ The capacity of *inductive reasoning* is the logical thought process that moves from the part to an understanding of the whole. In philosophy, this is called the *Aristotelian method.* Jessica Fletcher uses it in "Murder She Wrote." She spends the entire show gathering clues to determine who committed a murder. In the last five minutes of the program, she masterfully puts the clues together and figures out who the murderer is.

■ The capacity of **deductive reasoning** is the logical thought process that moves from the whole to an understanding of the parts. In philosophy, this is called the *Platonic method*. Colombo uses this capacity in the TV show of the same name. At the beginning of the show, he knows who committed the murder. He then spends the remainder of the show gathering the evidence to prove it.

■ Developing your capacities to **discern relationships and connections** will help you sort through and make sense out of the increasingly complex data that bombard you every day. This capacity involves being able to evaluate this montage of information and find those things that link, conjoin, and commingle, and that are associated with other things that are meaningful and important to you, and to discard the rest.

■ The capacity of **performing complex calculations** is the area most of us have traditionally and probably associated exclusively with logical-mathematical intelligence. However, this capacity goes far beyond what we learned in school Yes, it does involve the capacity to deal with numerical relationships and mathematical processes and operations, but it also involves the ability to utilize these things in everyday, practical living!

■ **Scientific reasoning** is a capacity that is in no way limited to pure scientific pursuits! The basic scientific method is the process of observing, judging, weighing up, deciding, and acting. Every time you successfully solve a problem you are facing in your life you use the "scientific" method. You first of all observe all of the facts related to your problem. Next you make a judgment about which facts are relevant to determine which are *most* relevant to the problem you are trying to solve. You then make a decision about the logical course of action. And, finally, you act on it!

## The Object-Free Intelligences

These intelligences are triggered by the structures and patterns of particular languages and sound as well as by all the various features and possibilities of the auditory and oral systems. These intelligences do not rely on objects, real or imagined, that have an independent existence in the external world or the world of the imagination. The triggering phenomenon instead involves such things as an author's or poet's creation using the written word; the evocative power of a musical composition; the power of the spoken word to inspire, motivate, or move us to action; and the impact of the auditory realm of sound, vibrational patterns, tones, beats, and rhythm.

## Verbal-Linguistic Intelligence

This intelligence is probably the most familiar and well known to us in the Western world. Most of us spend the majority of time during our waking hours using verbal-linguistic intelligence. It is one of the main emphases of all our systems of public education. It involves all forms of language, including the ability to read the newspaper, a novel, labels on various products we buy, and so on; the ability to write essays, poetry, reports, letters, and so on; formal speaking before an audience and informal conversation with a friend; and it involves listening to the words of others and understanding what they are both saying and intending to communicate.

Think for a moment about the miracle of language. There was a time that our human verbal communication was exclusively a matter of grunts, groans, screams, and other sounds produced by our vocal chords. In our individual human development, we start out in much the same way, communicating our needs through grunts, groans, infant babbling and cooing, and yes, also often screaming at the top of our lungs in an effort to get our needs met. How does this primordial cacophony transform itself into the high-level, subtle linguistic ability that we almost take for granted in our society? How do we move from grunts, groans, and babblings to the acquisition of such sophisticated skills as eloquent public speaking, the ability to produce a wide range of literature—poetry, drama, essays, epic stories—that deeply touches the lives of other people? How do we learn to interpret various abstract scratchings on a piece of paper as meaningful communication from others?

According to contemporary brain research, we possess at birth the capacity to speak more than three thousand different languages; however we are not born proficient in any of them. When we begin to interact with the primary language in our environment, the brain can already recognize all of the sounds of the language. The language networks in our brain, through cultural patterning, frequency of hearing, repeated attempts to mimic these sounds, and probably our own survival instincts as well, usually cause us to develop fully only one or two of these potential languages into a full-blown, sophisticated language system.

The primary language center of the brain is called Broca's area. Within Broca's area, at least four distinct neurological processes occur that are involved in the development of our verbal-linguistic intelligence capacities. The first capacity is the *syntactic process* (or syntax),which is the ability to understand the culturally agreed-on logic of a given language system. When you were in school, were you assigned endless grammar drills that were meant to get you clear on subject and verb agreement, speaking and writing with clear antecedents, avoiding dangling participles, making sure prepositional phrases had an object, and so on? Also involved in this process is understanding the order, meaning, and relationships of words in a sentence, sentences in a paragraph, and paragraphs in an essay.

The second process that occurs in Broca's area is the *phonetic process* (or phonics), which is the ability to process language meanings through the tones, pitch, timbre, and rhythmic patterns of verbal communication; namely, *how* something is said often communicates more than the actual meaning of *what* is said! Think about the experience of the literal meaning of someone's speaking is out of synch with how they are saying it; for example, ***"No, I am not upset!!!"***

The third is the *semantic process* (or semantics), which is the ability to discern the various shades of meanings of different words. It involves skill in careful linguistic analysis. You can most clearly observe this process in the creative work of poets, public speakers, or motivational writers, searching (sometimes for weeks!) for a single phrase that will embody precisely what they intend to communicate to a reader or listener. It involves skillful use of such things as metaphor, simile, hyperbole, analogy, and symbolic language.

The fourth neurological operation is the **praxis process,** the ability to understand cultural nuances, idioms, and the actual practical meanings of words and phrases in a variety of changing sociocultural settings. Consider for a moment some of the differences between British English and American English: a *lift* in British English is an elevator, a *nappy* is a diaper, and *first floor* in a building refers to what American English calls the second floor. Consider the differences even within American English, depending on the part of the country where you are: a *bubbler* is a drinking fountain on the East Coast; if you order a "soda" in a restaurant in various parts of America you may get totally different drinks!

Let's do a quick inventory of the core capacities that comprise verbal-linguistic intelligence:

- The capacity to ***understand the order and meaning of words*** is the very complex process of grasping word meanings in a given context and knowing how to shift both meaning and context by rearranging words. For example, how many sentences, each with a different meaning, can you create by simply rearranging the ten words in the sentence "The man only wanted to tell the child about this"?

- ***Explaining, teaching, and learning*** mean being able to give accurate verbal or written instructions to another and being able to follow such instructions given to you. This capacity involves not only thoroughly understanding what you are trying to explain or teach, but also understanding what another will hear and understand in your instructions. How many times have you been stumped by the supposedly "easy to follow" instructions in a product manual? For example, remember trying to connect your VCR to your TV, then trying to figure out how to program it to record a program on one channel while you are watching something on another channel?

- ***Linguistically based humor*** deals with such things as plays on words (puns) and the play with words (the story with the surprise ending, riddles, jokes that usually involve various "twists" of the language or misunderstood words and phrases, limericks, double-meanings, and so on). Also involved is an understanding of the setting in which something is funny. The sociocultural context of humor is important to understand; something that is funny in one situation may be an insult another.

■ Think about the skill of politicians, ministers, social activists, speakers at charity fundraisers, or TV announcers who ***convince others of a course of action*** or who use persuasive speaking and writing. It involves the development of great sensitivity to the subtle meanings of the language and the sounds and rhythms of speech, as well as an understanding of the linguistic context of the listener. It involves an understanding of emphasis in speaking to underscore the most important parts of your communication. It is the ability to use the spoken and written word to influence and motivate people.

■ The capacity of ***memory and recall*** is the ability to access verbally stored information from the brain's short- and long-term memory, which involves a wide variety of techniques specific to an individual. How do you remember an address or people's names when you're in a group? What is your technique to recall information from something you read three weeks ago when you need to produce it in a current conversation? What is your strategy for finding the words you need to complete a crossword puzzle or a word jumble?

■ Possibly one of the most interesting and profound aspects of this intelligence is its capacity to engage ***metalinguistic analysis.*** This unique ability is the use of language to investigate language. Think about times when you are talking with another person and you are confused. How do you gain clarity? You probably use language to ask about his or her use of language: "Do you mean this or do you mean that?" Persons involved in a debate will use language to destroy the language-based argument of an opponent, or attorneys will use language to further investigate the also verbal testimony of a witness on the stand.

## Auditory-Vibrational (Musical-Rhythmic) Intelligence

I have started to call this intelligence the auditory-vibrational intelligences for, cognitively, it goes way beyond music and rhythm in their own right. It is really dealing with the whole realm of sound, vibration, tones, beats, and so on. We know many things by simply listening to the sounds around us. For example, part of the year I live in Chicago, right in the city. When I am preparing to go someplace in the city, I can step out onto my patio and listen to the traffic patterns on the street and know instantly if I should drive my own car or take public transportation. Think what you can tell about the weather by listening to what is happening outside—the howling wind, the pitter-patter of rain, the sudden clap of thunder. When you are talking with another person or listening to others converse, think about how much you can learn by simply listening to the tone and pitch of their voice and the rhythms of their speech. We can tell when they are happy or joyful. We can tell when they are uptight or angry, when they are relaxed and comfortable, when they are very excited about what they are sharing. You can tell if something is wrong with your car, even if you don't know what it is. Can you tell who is approaching by listening to the sound of footsteps? Or maybe, if you are a parent, you can tell who is at home in your house and what they are doing just by the sounds of their movements and activities.

From a neurological perspective, this intelligence is the first of our intelligences to develop. Think for a moment about the world of sound and rhythm in which we are immersed while still in the womb. We hear our mother's heartbeat as well as the whole range of other body functions from digestion to inhalation and exhalation. In utero we also hear voices in the external world, including those of people strongly expressing their opinions in a debate, different types of conversation on TV shows and movies, people laughing at a good joke, and the sound of someone crying. We hear a wide range of sounds from the environment outside our homes: the sound of blaring horns during rush hour traffic; the sound of a dog barking; the sirens of emergency vehicles; and the sound of various forms of public transportation—trains, buses, airplanes. And just consider the experience of rhythm in this prenatal world. Every movement our mother makes creates a different rhythm or beat that we unavoidably experience. Much of this intelligence is patterned in our brains long before we are actually born!

Of all the eight intelligences, the consciousness-altering effects of music, rhythm, sound, and vibration are more powerful than the effects of any of the other intelligences. Just think of the power of these effects to shift our moods, inspire religious devotion, evoke national pride, express deep love for another, or deep loss and grief. Consider the power of music, rhythm, sound, and vibration when you are watching a TV show or a movie; they are used to help us anticipate what will happen next or to enhance and amplify the action in a particular scene. I have also been fascinated over the years with the development of the auditory-vibrational intelligence in people who are profoundly deaf. Often their capacities to "hear" through vibrational patterns have been developed to very high levels of cognitive processing. Beyond hearing, our auditory organs serve at least two other critical functions in our lives: they provide us with our sense of balance and also with our sense of laterality and spatiality; namely time/space coordination.

The language and operating modality of musical-rhythmic intelligence are the language of sound, including sounds from the environment, human-produced sounds, sounds made by machines, and sounds that come from musical instruments. In addition to the experience of sound (which is heard), the language of this intelligence involves rhythms, beats, and vibrational patterns (which are felt and experienced in the body).

Let's do a quick inventory of the core capacities that are part of musical-rhythmic intelligence:

- The evocative power of music and rhythm is very profound. Certain kinds of music and rhythm can calm us, energize us, make us feel anxious, and so on. Developing an ***appreciation for the structure of music and rhythm*** and its affective qualities is one of the ways to strengthen your musical-rhythmic intelligence.

- We have certain ***schemas or frames for hearing music*** in our minds. We make conscious and unconscious connections with various kinds of music and rhythm. Think about times when you are watching a movie or TV show and you anticipate what is about to happen by listening to the music. What kinds of music and rhythm do you associate with a chase scene or a fight scene? What music do you associate with the circus? Or with various products advertised on TV or the radio?

■ *Sensitivity to sounds* deals with "turning up" our hearing capacities and learning to process the wide variety of auditory stimuli that have an impact on us every day of our lives. Just think what you can learn by listening to the sound of someone's footsteps and what you can learn by listening to the sounds of the traffic outside or to the sounds of various weather conditions!

■ *Recognition, creation, and reproduction of melody, rhythm, and sound* comprise the capacity to repeat accurately or mimic a tonal or rhythmic pattern produced by another person. We probably most often exercise this capacity when we're trying to sing a new hymn at church, or when learning a new dance step and we're trying to get an internal feel for the beat of the music.

■ The capacity for *utilizing various characteristic qualities of tones and rhythm* as a way to enhance and deepen communication is a powerful aspect of this intelligence. What tonal qualities of speech do you associate with boredom, excitement, fear, surprise, and contentment? What rhythms do you associate with various cultures; for example the beat of Latin America or the beat of an American Indian culture? What are the sounds you associate with the busy downtown area of the city, and what do you associate with being in a rural area?

## The Personal Intelligences

At the heart of both inter- and intrapersonal intelligences are our own lives; on the one hand, our lives in relationship with each other; on the other, our lives as individuals. It is these personal elements that trigger these intelligences. In some ways these intelligences are flip sides of a single coin. Often the greatest learning and discoveries about the self happen when we are working with or playing with others as part of some collaborative effort, be it a game, a community project, or a committee on which we are serving. The reverse is also true. Those things we know *deeply* about the self we are fairly safe to assume are also true about others; namely, once you get through the many layers of a personality, you arrive at a *core self* in which there are many more similarities than differences!

## Interpersonal Intelligence

What great experiences have you had as part of a team, whether it was a sports team, a team in the workplace, or a group project in an organization? Can you think of important things you have learned from working with others? When has another person spent time with you helping you understand or teaching you something? Can you remember completing a task or project that you could not have completed on your own, when you had to rely on another person or other people? These experiences are the "stuff" of interpersonal intelligence, the "stuff" of human relating, collaborating with others, and learning from and about other people.

We spend a large amount of every day working with and relating to other people without really thinking about it. Yet, how skillful are we in this relating? How much do we really value and understand everything that is involved in the depth of cooperation and collaboration with others? Beginning in early childhood, throughout our formal schooling, and into our adult work life, the normal socialization process of most Western societies provides us with hundreds of both formal and informal training opportunities in how to be competitive and in being the "rugged individual."

There is nothing whatsoever wrong with competition or individualism, if we keep them in perspective. In fact, in some ways they are survival skills, especially in capitalistic, free-enterprise societies. However, the interpersonal capacities of cooperation and collaboration are quite different from those of competition and individualism. Had you grown up in a tribal society, or a culture in which the family and extended family was the core social unit, you would likely have acquired the capacities of interpersonal intelligence in much the same way people learned to compete or stand on their own two feet in Western societies.

Let's do a quick inventory of the core capacities that comprise interpersonal intelligence:

- The capacity of ***effective verbal and nonverbal*** communication with others goes way beyond the simple meanings of the words we use. Think about times when someone's body language or the tone and rhythm of voice were out of synch with what they were saying.

■ When talking with others, can you tell when they are upset? Can you tell when they are feeling uncomfortable or when they are excited? Can you sense when they are bored, preoccupied with something else, or when they have a hidden agenda? The capacity to accurately **read others' moods, temperaments, motivations, and feelings** is a key to effective and meaningful interpersonal encounters.

■ Recall times when you were part of a team, the success of which required that each member did a part. The capacity of **working cooperatively in a group** deals with learning how to do your part and allowing others to do theirs for the sake of the group goal.

■ In everyday communication, we often miss what another is saying because our own internal mind chatter gets in the way. **Listening to another's perspective** is the capacity to listen fully and deeply to another, and to shut off temporarily the inner mental commentary, planning our comments or rebuttal, or thinking about a witty response to what is being said.

■ **Passing into the life of another** is the capacity to empathize with another's perspective, feelings, values, and beliefs, *especially* when they are somewhat foreign to our own. This capacity does not necessarily mean *agreeing* with the other's perspective. But it does mean *understanding* and *appreciating* the other perspective.

■ Recall times when you were part of a group effort and the final product was greater than the mere sum of the individual contributions of the various members of the group. This is called *synergy* (from the Greek *syn* and *ergos*), which means a "spontaneous working together." The capacity to **create and maintain synergy** in a group is one of the capacities of interpersonal intelligence.

## Intrapersonal Intelligence

As far as we know, human beings are the only creatures who possess self-consciousness, the ability to step back from ourselves, to reflect on the self, and to learn from our reflection. See if you can recognize this process in your life: When you are alone, what nonwork-related thinking do you really enjoy? What do you do for personal renewal? When you are stressed, angry, or anxious, what practices do you use to alter your consciousness or awareness? In the last year, what new discoveries have you made about yourself that in some way altered your previous self-understanding? If you had to answer the question "Who am I really?" and you couldn't talk about external appearances, skills you've acquired, relationships you have with others, or your work, what would you say? What do you do when you need inspiration or when you need to spark your own creativity? What is the process you use to evaluate yourself and your goals? What personal growth and development activities do you currently do, or what have you tried in the recent past? The "stuff" of intrapersonal intelligence is the "stuff" of self-awareness and self-reflection, and being in touch with the inner world of our individual being.

Intrapersonal intelligence is probably the least understood of the eight intelligences, the least valued in our Western world, and often the most feared, possibly because many consider it to be dangerous. Why? Part of the problem comes from the fact that a great deal of the work of this intelligence occurs deep within the human psyche; therefore, we have no "external product" to show for this work, and we are a product-driven society! Another part of the problem is that all Western societies favor verbal-linguistic and logical-mathematical intelligence: "If you can't write about it, talk about it, and logically explain it to someone else, it has no real value." However some of our intrapersonal knowings can't be adequately communicated in these verbal-linguistic or logical-mathematical forms. Have you noticed how we feel we must have some form of external stimulation to keep us entertained almost every waking hour? And how we hesitate to take the time to look deeply into the self?

Let's do a quick inventory of the core capacities that comprise intrapersonal intelligence:

- The capacity to **concentrate** is being able to bring the mind to a single point of focus and hold it there. Think about times when you really got caught up in a novel and were able to block out everything else going on around you.

■ *Mindfulness* is the exact opposite of mindlessness, but it is another capacity that falls under intrapersonal intelligence. So much of our lives are spent on automatic pilot, but this capacity is about training yourself to stop, pay attention, and appreciate the minute details of even the most mundane experiences.

■ *Metacognition* is the activity of thinking about thinking. Do you have inner conversations with yourself? Think about when you have a problem to solve: do you sometimes talk yourself through it? When you go to the store, do you talk to yourself about things you need to remember to pick up? Do you ever analyze your thinking with the hopes of improving it? Good news! This is not early senility setting in. It is metacognition!

■ Think about the mood swings of a normal day. Do you know what things tend to bring you a high and what brings you low? Developing your capacities of *awareness and expression of various feelings* helps you "get a grip" on this dynamic and take charge of your feelings rather than let them run you.

■ *Transpersonal sense of the self* is the capacity to identify and appreciate the self that goes beyond the self as an isolated, solitary entity unto itself. Yes, we are all individuals, but that is not the whole story! We are also part of other people and they are part of us, and we are part of the universe and it is part of us!

■ There are levels within levels within levels to our thinking/reasoning processes. *Higher-order thinking and reasoning* comprise the capacity to move your thinking consciously from "the facts ma'am, nothing but the facts" to an awareness of your thinking process itself to the higher-order ability to integrate learning and use it in everyday life.

If you are feeling a bit overwhelmed at this point, don't worry. In the chapters that follow, I demonstrate ways to work with these capacities in and through the curriculum itself. However, if you are feeling the need for more work in understanding the capacities or, even more important, on enhancing and further developing and strengthening your own capacities, I invite you to explore other resources. *Intelligence Builders for Every Student* provides a sampling of exercises adapted for use with students. You can also find a discussion of the capacities with exercises for awakening and strengthing them in *Eight Ways of Knowing*.

# 3

# The Year-Long Curriculum Journey

*To the young mind every thing is individual, stands by itself. By and by it finds how to join two things and see in them one nature; then three, then three thousand; and so, tyrannized over by its own unifying instinct, it goes on tying things together, diminishing anomalies, discovering roots running underground whereby contrary and remote things cohere and flower out from one stem . . . The astronomer discovers that geometry, a pure abstraction of the human mind, is the measure of planetary motion. The chemist finds proportions and intelligible method throughout matter; and science is nothing but the finding of analogy, identity, in the most remote parts.*

—Ralph Waldo Emerson

This model is based on work I did with a curriculum integration task force in El Paso, Texas, a number of years ago. I was invited to work with the task force over a period of several weeks during which they received in-depth training in the practical applications of the theory of multiple intelligences, more specifically, in the application of MI to integrating the curriculum of the district. The goal was to take the curriculum manuals of the district, K through 12, and rewrite them to incorporate the various capacities of the intelligences into the existing curriculum.

## Purpose of the Year-Long Curriculum Journey

The intent of the Year-Long Curriculum Journey model is to embed all the capacities of all the intelligences in the content of the existing curriculum. The model calls for intersecting the various aspects of the curriculum with the capacities of the intelligences.

## Goals of the Year-Long Curriculum Journey

- To provide multiple opportunities, throughout the year, in and through the existing curriculum, for students to use and develop the full range of their intelligence capacities. As with any skill we have developed in our lives, considerable and repeated practice is often involved.

- To deepen students' understanding of curricular concepts by learning to present these concepts using a variety of the intelligences.

- To provide a focus for integrating MI into the curriculum for a school faculty or district/school division task force.

## The Development of the Year-Long Curriculum Journey

The task force in El Paso worked with a matrix (see examples on pages 55–69) on which the year's curriculum subjects were listed across the top and the intelligences down the side. We then examined each capacity, looking across the curriculum to find many places to fit it in without making it too contrived, much like a teacher interested in a whole language approach to the language arts would look for ways to incorporate literature.

We would take a curricular area—for example, math—and ask ourselves, "Where in and through the curriculum, as it is already designed, do we see opportunities to help students practice using the visual-spatial capacity to **form mental images?** We listed all the places where this capacity could be employed in the actual teaching and learning. We had the same conversation about **graphic representation, recognizing relationships between objects in space,** and so on, until we had found a place for all of the visual-spatial capacities in the curriculum. Then we took another intelligence—say, bodily-kinesthetic—and continued the process, seeking all the places where we could embed its capacities in the existing curriculum. The task force continued until all of the capacities of all the intelligences had found their home in all of the areas of the curriculum.

Obviously, this process is very lengthy and involved. Of all of the integration models presented in this book, the Year-Long Curriculum is the most difficult to work with because of the amount of time required to do it well. It also requires a cross-school or cross-district/division commitment to work effectively. However, of all the models presented, I believe it offers the greatest potential for in-depth, long-lasting change.

One of the teachers involved in the El Paso task force brought home this point most powerfully. At one point during the time we were working on this project, she suddenly leapt out of her seat and said, "*Wow!* Do you see what we have done here? We have set new standards for ourselves as teachers—standards that require us to help students develop all that they can be intellectually!" She asked, "Can you imagine how long a teacher would last in our district (or in any district anywhere!) if one year he or she said, 'Well, I'm a bit tired of the language arts stuff and, anyway, I'm not very strong at it, so I'm going to let someone else work on developing those skills in my students this year'?" She continued by making a poignant comparison: "Yet we let ourselves get by with this attitude in other intelligence areas, such as musical-rhythmic intelligence! We'll say, 'That's the job of the music teacher.' Or, in the case of bodily-kinesthetic intelligence, 'That's why they go to PE or why they have recess'!"

Her point is very powerful if we are concerned with *real* curricular reform and renewal as opposed to simply moving around the existing pieces in a new fashion. When we value the development of all the capacities of all the intelligences, students begin to feel comfortable working in the various intelligence areas, but more important, they begin to more fully realize their intellectual potential as human beings. I feel it is a copout on our part if we allow the intelligences to be isolated into curriculum areas, for example, suggesting that developing visual-spatial intelligence is really the art instructor's job. Such is no more the case than is developing verbal-linguistic capacities only when we are dealing with the language arts part of the curriculum! In the work with this model in El Paso, basically all teachers, regardless of specific subject areas, began to see themselves as responsible for helping students develop all the capacities of all the intelligences, many of which in the past had been relegated to the fine arts curriculum.

## Things about This Model That Excite and Interest Me

- *It does* not *suggest that you add a bunch of new stuff to the curriculum.* In every district where I have worked, teachers feel there is already too much stuff in the curriculum to get through in a year. Rather, in and through the existing stuff of the curriculum, we can find ways to help students practice using the various capacities of the intelligences.

- *It applies to a variety of curriculum integration approaches.* In the examples I share are ways to use the model with an individual, subject-focused curriculum; with an interdisciplinary, thematic curriculum; and with a specific departmental curriculum, which is generally more prevalent in secondary education. While philosophically I am of the persuasion that the integrated, interdisciplinary, thematic approach is most effective in helping students make deep connections between the curriculum and their lives, I wanted to show that the Year-Long model can work with almost any curricular approach.

- *It applies to the entire curricular journey of a district, K through 12.* Teachers and administrators often mistakenly assume that MI is fine for students in the elementary years and that it works best with them. But when they get into middle school, junior high, or high school, everything must change to "preparing them for the *real world.*"

Unfortunately, as educators, we are frequently not in touch with the actual requirements of success in the so-called real world. Skill in the verbal-linguistic and logical-mathematical intelligences does not guarantee one's success either in college or in the workplace. Yes, every college wants students and every employer wants employees who can read, write, and do 'rithmetic, but they also want people who have good people skills, who can effectively function as part of a team, who are creative problem solvers, who can set goals for themselves, who are able to self-evaluate and make corrections, and so on.

■ *It integrates the curriculum with the intelligences as the integrator.* There are some similarities to all fine arts integrated curriculum currently being approved in a number of districts and divisions. However, I must reiterate that in the first instance there are no direct *curricular content* implications between the theory of multiple intelligences and what is taught in a system of formal education. Now, yes, I do believe that we must make major content changes given the amazing times in which we are living. However, this model is not based on content and thus can be used regardless of any specific content. It simply suggests that all teachers, in and through all curricular content, provide students opportunities to practice using all the intelligences. In so doing students will not only better understand and master the curriculum, but will also more fully develop, strengthen, and enhance the various intelligences within themselves.

## The Basic Process

Following are steps for using the "Year-Long Curriculum Journey" work sheet (please refer to the examples on pages 55–69):

Step 1 Determine the time frame with which you will work: a term, the entire year, a specific number of weeks. Articulate your instructional objectives and outcomes for the various content areas your students will realize during time frame.

**Step 2** Across the top of the chart, list each general curriculum content area you'll be addressing during the time frame. Be as specific or as general as you want. For example, if one of the top curricular categories is something as general as "math," what you'll be doing is brainstorming all of the potential ways you can incorporate the capacities to help students process the information you will be covering. If the heading is more specific, such as "fractions," you'll be looking for ways to incorporate the capacities into that extended unit and its related content.

**Step 3** In the first column, list the intelligences and their related capacities from the MI Capacities Wheels (pages 19 and 20). In the work sheets, I have included an individual chart for each intelligence, with some standard curriculum areas across the top to get you started. Since your ultimate goal is to embed *all of the capacities* for *all of the intelligences* in the content areas, this work sheet gives you a lot of space and encourages you to write a lot of ideas under each one. *Note that, in my examples, I have taken only one capacity for each intelligence to illustrate how to fill out the work sheets.*

**Step 4** Think about all of the concepts, skills, operations, principles, facts and figures, and so on that are involved in mastering the particular content area listed in the top row. Intersect the different capacities with the content and see what ideas occur to you. Ask, "Where can I use this capacity to enhance students' understanding of what I am covering?" Don't work in a linear fashion. Jump all over the chart, as if it were an electric grid with various areas lighting up randomly, filling in any intersection that "lights up." If you get stuck in coming up with ideas for one capacity, move on to another and work with it for a while.

The most difficult part of working with this chart is that you are not doing lesson planning per se. Rather, you are looking for things you can repeat many times throughout the year. Remember, it takes repeated practice of working with a capacity to really develop skill in using it. Therefore, as you ask yourself the question concerning where to use a given capacity to amplify students' learning, ask, for example, "Where are *all* the places graphic representation could be used to help students understand?" Your answer might be, "I can use graphic representation to help students understand settings and characters in stories (language arts), to help them understand fractional parts (math), or to help them understand their observations in lab experiments (science)."

**Step 5**  Once you have completed the charts, use them when you are planning daily lessons to make sure that you include the capacities in your instruction and in the learning tasks you design for your students.

## Evaluations of the Model

Following are some of my own thoughts about the pluses and minuses of the Year-Long Curriculum Journey model. I hope you and your colleagues will engage in a similar evaluation of this model in your department, school, district, or school division to find the approach that is best suited to your situation.

### + + + PLUSES + + +

▶ **Once completed, it becomes part and parcel of the curriculum.** When you have completed the task that this model suggests, suddenly the job of helping students use all of their intellectual capacities to master the curriculum is no longer a big deal. The MI capacities become part and parcel of the curriculum. Likewise, other than making minor adjustments and adaptations to changes in the content, you will likely not need to do this job on this scale again, but can reuse the charts from year to year.

▶ **It is dynamic.** Lights will continue to go on for you as you move into the lesson planning phase of the model and as you implement the capacities you have noted. Students will also come up with their own ideas about capacities they can use, and you can add these to your chart as the term progresses.

▶ **It creates new standards for teaching.** As the teacher in El Paso pointed out, in some regards, this model is as much about transforming instructional practice and standards as anything else. A school, district, or school division that adopts this approach of integrating MI into the curriculum consciously or unconsciously makes the decision that *one of the most important things we can do for students is to provide them with opportunities, in and through the curriculum, to enhance, strengthen, and develop their full intellectual potential.* The importance of this task is at least equal to the mastery of "curricular stuff."

▶ **New standards for student learning.** The adoption of the Year-Long Curriculum Journey approach raises the educational standards of a school, school district, or school division in that it *promotes students' deeper understanding, assimilation, and integration of the curriculum.* This model does not allow those students who are good with words to get by without showing genuine understanding that goes beyond words. Conversely, those who are not verbally or logically strong still have opportunities to succeed by using all their intelligences. What is more, we have a way to use their strong intelligences to develop strength in their weaker intelligences, including the verbal-linguistic area.

▶ **It creates a common vision for a school, district, or school division.** In some ways, once MI has been integrated into the curriculum in this way, you have an implicit mission statement in place; namely, to help students develop their full intelligence *and* to use all the intelligences to help students master and understand the curriculum. People will have worked together to create this reality and possibility in and through the curriculum, and so it will be a part of their being.

## – – – MINUSES – – –

▶ **It is time consuming.** As I mentioned earlier, this model involves a lengthy process of not only thoroughly understanding the curriculum and reasons for each part of it, but also thoroughly understanding the capacities of the intelligences. You must understand how to tap into and utilize them to help students grasp the required material and exercise their many ways of knowing. You must be willing to play with the capacities and to explore their potential uses with the existing curriculum. And of course, the curricular use of some of the capacities is more obvious than others. I believe that if we give ourselves the time to work back and forth between the curriculum and the capacities, we will discover some tremendously exciting things about both. Once it's done, it's done for a long time; you don't have to make the same time commitment each year or term that you do in the beginning, and you have a most effective tool with which to work.

▶ **It requires large "buy in" across school, district, or division.** I already mentioned that this model assumes a thorough commitment from all staff members. It cannot be mandated from the top down, nor completed by one person and handed to teachers to implement. People must understand the approach, what it will do for students and teachers, and how it will benefit the district or school division. They must also be willing to put in the time to make it happen. Everyone must work together to make it happen. However, when people do work together on something this profound and this important, and when all of their input is valued, the synergy that can result can solidify staff relationships, making everyone feel part of a vital team whose goal is to teach students in a way that ensures lifelong love of learning.

▶ **Parents can misunderstand.** As with every other minus, this one has a positive side, as well. If parents do not understand the intelligences and how they can help students in their schooling, including getting them ready for college and "life in the real world," you will likely experience a fair amount of resistance; many parents will initially feel that working with the MI capacities in this fashion takes time away from the "real stuff of school," namely, reading, writing, and 'rithmetic. However, use of this model almost requires that we take time to inservice parents and help them understand. In my experience of working with many parent groups over the years, I have found that in some ways parents already unconsciously know that their children are smart in many more ways than school has traditionally valued. When we take the time to let them see that we are now valuing the many ways their kids are smart and, what is more, using all of these ways of knowing to help them succeed in school and beyond, most parents will instantly get on board, so to speak.

# Year-Long Curriculum Journey
## *Elementary*

## Focus on Individual Subjects

This example illustrates how to use the Year-Long Curriculum Journey with a traditional approach to the various subject areas that are frequently part of the elementary school journey. I am not suggesting that there is no cross-fertilization between the subjects. However, this example, for the sake of demonstration, assumes that each subject area is self-contained.

## Academic Objectives and Outcomes

These objectives and outcomes are related to the aspects of each subject area included in the chart rather than the entire year's objectives and outcomes.

### Language Arts

- To understand the various elements of a variety of literature: characters, plot, vocabulary, and settings in a story; main points of an essay; figures of speech in poetry

### Mathematics

- To explore and understand a variety of math processes and distinct operations: the processes of addition, subtraction, multiplication, and division; distinct operations such as carrying and borrowing, place value, decimals and fractions

### Science and Health

- To deepen understanding of basic scientific concepts and processes: states of matter, parts of a cell, classification of living things

- To understand the key principles of healthy living, including diet, exercise, avoiding substance abuse

### Global Studies and History

- To understand various world cultures, different historical eras, and ways they have shaped our lives today: causes of major historical events and events within different nations; key figures and their influence; environmental, geographical, climatic differences in our world; and so on.

### Practical Arts

- To learn how to use a variety of practical skills including physical education skills, preparing meals, building things, safety in everyday life, and so on.

### Fine Arts (dance, drama, instrumental and vocal music, art)

- To rehearse and strengthen one's skill in the various fine arts areas

● To understand specific content of such things as instrumental music, dance, drama, and so on

● To make connections between the fine arts and the rest of the school curriculum

These objectives and outcomes are necessarily somewhat general, given that we are dealing with curriculum pieces that, in principle, span an entire term or longer. Also, my intention is to provide a generic example (pages 55–56) to demonstrate how you can use this model with curriculum that is typically part of the elementary years. When you go through the process yourself, my general example will help you hone and more clearly focus the term's objectives and outcomes for the different subjects you are teaching. Please study the example before beginning.

## Commentary on the Elementary Year-Long Curriculum Journey Example

This focus on individual subjects in the curriculum assumes that during the day and week, you have scheduled distinct times for teaching each subject. The Year-Long Curriculum Journey is most useful for looking at these times. In some ways you are brainstorming all of the ways that the various MI capacities could be integrated into the teaching of this material. Once you have a plethora of ways you could incorporate the intelligences, select those capacities that seem most on target given your objectives and desired outcomes for the particulars you will be teaching in a given subject on a given day.

Following are some of my reflections, thoughts, insights, and other metacognitive postscripts and ramblings on this example.

■ While I do not believe that an isolated subject focus is the best way to approach curriculum development, I am also very much aware that this curriculum model is still what many school boards, parents, legislators, testing organizations, textbook companies, and the general public prefer. One cutting-edge approach to curriculum development today is the interdisciplinary or thematic approach. However, for whatever reasons, many schools are not there yet. This example of the Year-Long Curriculum Journey is very effective in that it reflects the reality of the curriculum as it exists now.

■ If a focus on individual subjects is what is required in your school, district, or school division, you can create a bit more *content integration* by tracing the common threads that run through the various subject areas, then incorporating the MI capacities into the development of those cross-curricular concepts. Work either with one capacity and apply it across the curriculum, or choose one concept and investigate ways to use various capacities in the various subjects.

■ Some teachers and administrators have found it more beneficial to use the Year-Long Curriculum Journey with the entire year's essential learnings or standards rather than with distinct subjects (or maybe *in addition to)*. Part of the value of working with incorporating the MI capacities with year-end standards and learning is that the multiple intelligences will help students achieve a much deeper understanding of the concepts and much higher levels of skill development. Rather than knowing and understanding the material in only one or two ways, they will know and understand in at least eight ways! We could adopt the following axiom: *The more ways something is known, the more it is known!*

■ Please also check out the middle school and high school examples; they demonstrate other approaches to using the Year-Long Curriculum Journey. Probably the most important thing to remember is that what goes in the top row of the chart (the curricular content) is totally flexible. The only fixed part is the first column, which deals with the intelligences. I call it fixed only because this model uses multiple intelligences to integrate the curriculum; therefore, it must remain the same to preserve the integrity of the model. However, you may find many ways to integrate MI as you work to apply the capacities across the curriculum.

# Year-Long Curriculum Journey for Elementary School

## Focus on Individual Subjects

| | Language Arts | Mathematics | Science and Health | Global Studies and History | Practical Arts (PE, home and industrial technology) | Fine Arts (dance, drama, instrumental and vocal music, visual art) |
|---|---|---|---|---|---|---|
| **Visual-Spatial** Capacity: graphic representation | Illustrate settings, characters, scenes, and so on, in literature and stories. | Create visual representations of story problems or numeric equations. | Draw, paint, or sculpt the stages of various scientific and health processes. | Create murals, dioramas, photograph displays of various cultures or stages of history. | Make posters, murals, and so on, to show steps of performing certain tasks or routines. | Create visual representations of various music, dance routines, or artistic processes. |
| **Logical-Mathematical** Capacity: graphic organizers | Create webs of main points of story, poems, or essays. | Use Venn diagrams to show similarities in and differences between various math processes. | List the steps in sequence of performing a science experiment and the results you come up with. | Rank key aspects that shaped a culture or the key causes of a historical event. | Make webs to explain ways to prepare a certain food, run a shop machine, manufacture a product, or perform an athletic skill. | Create a step-by-step time line that shows everything involved in completing a project. |
| **Naturalist** Capacity: recognizing and classifying species | Produce matrices that classify the interplay among characters and natural settings in a story. | Use plant or animal manipulatives from the natural world to solve varieties of math problems. | Create charts that show groups of various living things that are involved in the various units of study. | Analyze historical events or cultures based on the impact of natural phenomena. | Learn ways various categories of plants and animals are used to enhance everyday living, such as food, clothing, work, and so on. | Create a dance, painting, song, or drama based on regular living, and identifiable patterns in the natural world. |
| **Bodily-Kinesthetic** Capacity: mimetic abilities | Role-play scenes from a story or play or embody vocabulary, parts of speech, and so on. | Experiment with creating physical analogies to show various math processes or operations. | Create a dramatic enactment of scientific processes or of some health-related practice. | Reenact great moments from history or re-create the geophysical, socio-environment of another culture. | Demonstrate how to make a favorite snack, play a game, do a practical task. | Listen to songs and nursery rhymes that tell a story, and act them out as the story is shared with the class. |

# Year-Long Curriculum Journey for Elementary School

## Focus on Individual Subjects

| | Language Arts | Mathematics | Science and Health | Global Studies and History | Practical Arts (PE, home and industrial technology) | Fine Arts (dance, drama, instrumental and vocal music, visual art) |
|---|---|---|---|---|---|---|
| **Verbal-Linguistic** Capacity: linguistic humor | Substitute contemporary, famous figures for characters in a story. | Make up math concept, process, and operation riddles and limericks. | Create funny television stories based on various scientific processes or healthy living concepts. | Study jokes and funny stories from cultures different from your own, then discuss until you understand why they are funny in their cultural context. | Create role-plays that show what can go wrong when cooking a meal or making something. | Devise a dance routine, or write songs or musical compositions that use the unexpected to make people smile. |
| **Auditory-Vibrational** (Musical-Rhythmic) Capacity: auditory schemas and frames | Turn a piece of literature or poetry into a radio program with appropriate background sounds and music to match the story line. | Make various sounds that are analogous to the different stages in different math processes and operations. | Create an appropriate soundtrack to accompany and explain various scientific process and health concepts. | Listen to and learn to recognize the music, rhythms, and sounds from various historical eras or parts of the world. | Identify the correct sounds of such things as a well-tuned car engine, a computer booting up, various shop machines, and so on. | Recognize the sounds of various musical instruments or sections of a choir, or associate certain classical dance routines with music. |
| **Interpersonal** Capacity: working cooperatively in a group | Experiment with group writing projects in which individuals write a part of the story, then put the parts together to make a whole. | Design math problem-solving tasks that require a team effort and collaboration to solve. | Plan and execute science projects as part of a cooperative group. | Use the cooperative learning strategy jigsaw project to study a historical era or aspects of a culture. | Design a class event or project where students volunteer to do certain tasks (prepare a feast, make decorations, and so on). | Set up partners to build skills to enhance the development of various skills related to the disciplines. |
| **Intrapersonal** Capacity: higher-order thinking and reasoning | Reflect on characters or ideas presented in literature; in what ways do they inform us in the course of our daily living? | Identify places where math concepts, processes, and operations show up in life beyond the classroom and how they apply to practical daily living. | Ask "so what?" questions about various health and science-related concepts, processes, and facts. | Discuss and understand ways other historical eras and cultures have shaped and influenced modern life. | Create personal safety checklists for riding in a car, crossing the street, operating a computer, building something, cooking, and so on. | Use music, dance, art, or drama to express ways something learned in one subject is important in life today. |

## Interdisciplinary Thematic Unit on Energy

This example illustrates how to use the Year-Long Curriculum Journey with an interdisciplinary thematic unit on energy. The focus of the example is on the theme of energy. In the example, I have not concerned myself with the creation of the interdisciplinary aspects of the unit, which would involve teaching all subjects in and through one theme. My example shows instead how to embed the capacities of the intelligences into the exploration of a theme. However, I do make some suggestions regarding how to mesh the theme with the traditional disciplines of the school curriculum in the commentary that follows the example.

## Academic Objectives and Outcomes

- To understand a variety of sources of energy, including the history of each: how they were discovered; what geographical region they come from; key people, past and present, who are associated with each

- To understand the environmental impact of each source of energy and, when appropriate, what is currently being done to conserve the energy form and to minimize its impact on the larger environment

- To understand the raw form of the various energy sources and the process by which each is manufactured for human use, the byproducts of each, and various cost factors involved with each energy source

- To learn practical applications of various sources of energy and to determine which of those are best-suited for what jobs, how each has been used in the past, how each is used currently, and what possible future uses scientists are proposing

- To experiment with appropriate ways to use the various energy sources in life

After designing this unit, several other large energy forms occurred to me, including human and animal energy. One of the very interesting and exciting things about thematic units is that the boundaries of the content to be covered are often "leaky"; that is, they can often lead in some interesting and unexpected directions, especially if you are willing and able to pursue areas of interest that the theme sparks. In this case, for example, you could get into some of the more subtle forms of energy: the elements that energize human beings, mental energy, spiritual energy, psychic energy, the biorhythmic, natural energy fields on Earth created by the Moon, an earthquake, magnetic energy, cosmic energy, and so on. Please study the example on pages 62–63 before beginning.

## Commentary on the Middle School
## Year-Long Curriculum Journey Example

The interdisciplinary thematic unit approach assumes that all of the traditional subject areas such as language arts, math, science, social studies, and so on are fully covered as part of the exploration of a theme, *and* at the most appropriate times and places during the exploration. In some ways, given the assumptions of the Year-Long Curriculum Journey model, what you have is almost a double integration; you are not only embedding the intelligences into the curriculum, you are also embedding the traditional subject areas into the theme. For those who enjoy complexity, you could also have a third overlay: the year-end competencies and concept mastery that students need to attain in order to move on to the next grade level.

Following are some of my reflections, thoughts, insights, and other metacognitive postscripts and ramblings on this example.

■ The unit I have presented here could obviously be adapted to any thematic approach, whether the theme lasts for a whole year, a term, or for a shorter period of time. The key is to break the overall theme into its components or subthemes, then integrate the MI capacities into these. Again, as with the elementary example, you will need one chart for each intelligence, with the subthemes across the top and the capacities of the intelligences down the side. The work sheet is set up in this fashion, even though the example is not.

■ As I mentioned in the introduction of the unit, what I have presented is *not* what is usually meant by thematic integration. Usually one is concerned with exploring the theme in and through the various traditional disciplines. My main concern is to embed the MI capacities throughout the unit. However, if one puts on the eyeglasses of the traditional disciplines, numerous possibilities exist for covering the usual academic disciplines.

➤ Language arts would involve such things as learning the vocabulary of the various forms of energy, library or textbook research, written and oral reports on one's research findings, or guest speakers.

➤ Mathematics would involve students' calculating the amounts of energy needed for various tasks or figuring relative economic factors related to using each form of energy.

➤ Social studies would not only investigate the geographical locations of the natural resources that lead to the energy forms, but also the predominant forms of energy used in various parts of the world and how they shape the various cultures.

➤ Science is probably one of the most obvious connections as students explore energy as a naturally occurring phenomenon, but also as they learn about various ways to harness energy or refine it for humankind's use and benefit.

■ As I mentioned earlier, you also might find it useful to have another overlay that involves the knowledge and skills students must master by the end of the year, or what some provinces and school divisions in Canada are calling the "common essential learnings." The importance of this overlay is to make sure that in and through your exploration of the theme, students are in fact successfully mastering the knowledge and skills by which their academic progress will ultimately be judged.

■ One of the biggest "pluses" of the interdisciplinary thematic approach is that it tends to place all learning in context so that students are not learning a bunch of more or less isolated, unrelated facts, figures, processes, and so on. Rather, all the learning "fits together," so to speak. Learning becomes more holistic as students actively use the information they are learning to explore the theme further. The thematic approach is also tailor-made to go with the flow of students' interests, skills they want to develop, questions they have, and so on. You can still cover all of the major concepts, skills, and knowledge prescribed by the curriculum, but you are intrinsically motivating your learners as you do it.

■ I have known and worked with a number of elementary schools that have followed a theme for an entire year. More often than not, at the middle school level, I find that schools pursue a theme for a term. One of the most effective thematic approaches I've encountered was at a middle school in Wichita, Kansas. It elicited students' input on areas they would like to study and learn about during the year, then the teachers developed the themes based on the needs and desires of the students. Of course, this approach also created a great deal of student ownership because they were often involved in doing the necessary research on the theme and putting together presentations to share their research with one another.

# Year-Long Curriculum Journey for Middle School
## Interdisciplinary Theme Curriculum Focus: Energy

| | Water Energy | Wind Energy | Solar Energy | Steam Energy | Nuclear Energy | Fossil Fuels | Electric Energy |
|---|---|---|---|---|---|---|---|
| **Visual-Spatial** Capacity: active imagination | Look for patterns, designs, and images created by various sources of water energy (water wheel, dams, and so on). | Imagine that you are a feather or a leaf at the mercy of the wind; imagine all the things that can happen to you. | Play with sunlight to find ways to make various light patterns, designs, pictures or images. | Observe steam in various situations and note the differing patterns that occur; what do they remind you of? | Observe the various patterns of the atomic world under an electron microscope: What associations do you make? | Identify all the patterns of petroleum in its raw and refined state, for example, oil and water or the patterns within a combustion engine. | Observe the many patterns and designs that can be created with electricity, such as lightning, signs, and so on. |
| **Logical-Mathematical** Capacity: performing complex calculations | Calculate the volume and force of water needed to run various machines, to carry something downstream, and so on. | Decide whether windmills would work as a source of electricity in your neighborhood by calculating how much energy they would generate; make a case for or against using it as a source of energy. | With a magnifying glass, focus a sun's ray on a leaf. Figure out which of various angles of light burn the leaf soonest. | Figure out the amount of steam energy required to power a steam engine, steam iron, steam turbine, radiator, and to steam food, and so on. | Compare the cost factor differentials of nuclear energy and all other conceivable energy sources; analyze the comparative risk factors of each. | Learn how to figure such things as miles per gallon or liter of gas, the costs of using natural gas energy in the home, and so on. | Investigate the pros and cons of the use of electric energy in the home, in cars, and so on; include costs. |
| **Naturalist** Capacity: communion with nature | Spend time outdoors having as many experiences of water as a force in the natural world as you can. | Experience various kinds of wind, such as a storm, a cooling evening breeze, a zephyr. | Go outdoors and notice as many instances of the power of the sun (plants growing, fading light, and so on) as you can. | Take a field trip to places that you can experience the effects of steam on the environment, such as thermal springs, geysers, and so on. | Visit a nuclear power plant and view videos that illustrate nuclear energy being harnessed. | Study the journey of oil from its natural state to the variety of products in which it ends up; investigate environmental issues related to each. | Observe the various states of electricity, such as static, lightning, and so on, in the natural environment. |
| **Bodily-Kinesthetic** Capacity: mimetic abilities | Create a water dance that shows the uses of water energy and its potential harmful effects. | Role-play ways humans use the wind. | Act out the process of how the sun's rays get converted into usable energy. | With a group, create a human tableau that demonstrates ways various steam-driven machines and appliances function. | Create a physical demonstration that shows how nuclear energy works in a nuclear power plant. | Make up a physical game that incorporates the variety of states of petroleum and its various uses as an energy source. | Create a dance that shows the various ways humans have produced electrical power. |

# Year-Long Curriculum Journey for Middle School
## Interdisciplinary Theme Curriculum Focus: Energy

| | Water Energy | Wind Energy | Solar Energy | Steam Energy | Nuclear Energy | Fossil Fuels | Electric Energy |
|---|---|---|---|---|---|---|---|
| **Verbal-Linguistic** Capacity: explaining, teaching, and learning | Study the basic principles of water-driven technology and report your findings to other students. | Research ways scientists study wind as an energy source, then create a demonstration report that shares what you learned. | Study ways solar panels and batteries work, and create a display to explain your findings to others. | Investigate early humankind's discovery of and experiments with steam and explain how those evolved into a major source of energy today. | Explain the basic principles of how nuclear energy works. | Study the petroleum refining process and prepare reports on your finding. | Investigate the sources for electricity, including the other sources of energy in this unit. |
| **Auditory-Vibrational (Musical-Rhythmic)** Capacity: sensitivity to sound | Make audiotapes of the different sounds of water, then play them for others, asking them to guess what the water is doing. | Watch videos, TV shows, and movies, paying attention to the sound of the wind and how it is used to enhance the story. | Research the sound of the sun's energy from its source and ways solar energy is used to produce sound. | Explore the various sounds of steam and the variety of sounds that can be made using steam energy. | Listen to the sounds of the process of nuclear fission; learn how the energy that results from the process is harnessed. | Recognize the sounds that accompany the workings of each part of an internal combustion engine, and of gas passing through the engine. | Investigate ways an electric synthesizer works, and experiment with the various possibilities of electronically produced sound and music. |
| **Interpersonal** Capacity: listening to another's perspective | Share your experiences of the power of water with a partner, then your partner tells another about your experience, and that person tells another. | Talk with a partner about a variety of emotions (happy, sad, fearful, and so on), and listen to the energy of various breath patterns as your partner speaks. | Discuss and be able to repeat a partner's opinions on whether the nation should create a law that requires people to use solar energy. | With a partner or team, brainstorm ways we use steam in our everyday lives and how it makes our lives better. | With a partner, discuss the pros and cons of nuclear energy and be able to tell a third person what your partner thinks. | With a partner, take a viewpoint opposite your own on the issue of our shrinking oil supplies and stage a debate. | Reflect on all the terms based in electricity that shape our daily experience with others (giving someone "static," a "highly charged" discussion," and so on). Determine their origins. |
| **Intrapersonal** Capacity: mindfulness | List the many ways that the power of water is a part of your life, including positive and negative encounters with this energy. | Practice being acutely aware of the experience of wind in your life during the course of a normal day. | Block or unblock the sun's energy and light to experiment with creating a variety of moods. | Close your eyes and reflect on a typical day of your life: How is steam a part of each day, and how would your day be different without steam? | Do a risk-benefit analysis of nuclear energy: Do you think the risks outweigh the benefits, or vice versa? | Research to find out which petroleum-based products are part of your everyday life, including plastics, cars, and so on; explain how they contribute to and detract from your life. | List all the ways your life would be different without electrical energy, then compare your lists with a partner's. |

# *High School*

## Department Curriculum Focus

This example illustrates how to use the Year-Long Curriculum Journey with a high school department's curriculum. The example is language arts based, which, as I have suggested, could apply equally well to English and foreign language departments.

## Academic Objectives and Outcomes

These objectives and outcomes are related to the various aspects of the department's assumed curriculum for the year.

### Grammar (semantics, syntax, and praxis)

- To understand the various aspects involved in proper grammatical construction in both the spoken and written language, and to be able to demonstrate this understanding in and through their own writing.

### Poetry (various meters of poetry, forms of poetic expression, and figures of speech)

- To be able to analyze the structure and form of various types of poetry including the use of metaphor, simile, hyperbole, and so on, and to be able to create poetry that demonstrates various approaches and styles of poetic expression.

### Creative Writing (various forms and styles of writing)

- To understand various *styles* of writing, such as descriptive, declarative, interrogative, imperative, persuasive, and various *forms* of writing, such as essay, short story, news reports, and to be able to demonstrate both in their own creative writing.

### Literature (various genres, reading for understanding and meaning)

- To understand the structure and form of the various genres of literature, such as fable, short story, myth, epic poem, and be able to recognize each form as well as read and comprehend examples of each.

### Vocabulary (word definition, pronunciation, and spelling)

- To expand vocabulary, correct pronunciation, and use; to recognize new words in daily conversation and proper spelling and usage in writing.

### Formal Speaking and Conversation (types of formal speeches and styles of effective conversation with others)

- To master such skills as creating a formal presentation; delivering a variety of speeches (persuasive, demonstrative, expository); using a variety of presentation skills, (reading the audience and tailoring the speech, using appropriate body language, using humor); and listening and paraphrasing in informal conversation.

In reality, this example (pages 68–69) is probably slanted toward the English department. Nevertheless, with a slight turn of the dial, you can also accomplish most of what I suggest in the teaching and learning of a foreign language, especially if you alter the top-level content categories to more closely match your foreign language curriculum. Please study the example before beginning.

### Commentary on the High School Year-Long Curriculum Journey Example

Although I focused my example on the language arts departments (English and foreign language), I hope as you consider my suggestions, you will see how you can do the same thing with the curriculum in your content area. As in the other sections of this chapter, I recommend that you create a separate chart for each intelligence with the specific elements of the curriculum in the top row.

Following are some of my reflections, thoughts, insights, and other metacognitive postscripts and ramblings on this example:

- My example is not intended as a recommendation of what a department's curriculum *should* cover. Rather, I took material that is typically covered in English or foreign language classes to illustrate how to use this model. Regardless of your department or content area, remember that the task is to work with each capacity in each intelligence to incorporate or embed it into the existing curriculum. I use one capacity in each chart, but you can look to other examples throughout the book to get a feel for ways to incorporate other capacities. Start with the capacities that are more obviously connected to the content, then move to the less obvious ones.

- The example is my attempt to show ways to focus the content of the language arts department on *performance of the language*. However, regardless of your department, I believe this is one of the most beneficial things about this model: *it almost unavoidably moves students into the performance of their understanding and use of the knowledge in more or less real-world contexts.* This element is also one of the keys to authentic assessment of students' mastery of the curriculum.

■ It is very important that you take some time to teach high school students *about* multiple intelligences (see *Pathways of Learning* for suggestions). High school teachers often mistakenly assume that MI is good for the little kids, but believe that, at the high school level, there is not enough time to use MI given the demands of covering the content. However, I believe that, on the one hand, *there is more than one way to cover the content,* and on the other, if we are concerned with genuine *understanding* of the content we cover, the MI approach is the best way to go. Many high school teachers also assume that their students won't buy an MI approach. However, **if** students see us valuing and validating the intelligences, **if** we teach students about their own multiple ways of knowing, and **if** we work with the intelligences in ways that are developmentally appropriate, high school students will love the approach and beg to use it more often to help in their learning. Finally, high school teachers may believe that, because MI is not on the tests by which students will ultimately be judged, it's a waste of time. But while MI is not on the tests, if used appropriately, it can dramatically improve students' performances on tests, even when the performance required is biased toward verbal-linguistic and logical-mathematical intelligences.

■ As I'm sure you noticed, I do not address grade level specificity in the example. My goal was to demonstrate the use of this model with typical high school material that could occur at any level and probably does to one degree or another. You will obviously need to make appropriate adjustments depending on the academic level and skill of your students. Given the way the curriculum is often spiraled, you likely already revisit concepts you have taught in previous years by adding to the knowledge and skill base with each such revisiting. This model can be a powerful way to deepen and expand students' mastery of the concepts and skills in question each time they encounter them again.

# Year-Long Curriculum Journey for High School
## Focus on English or Foreign Language

| | Grammar (semantics, syntax, and praxis) | Poetry (meters, forms, and figures of speech) | Creative Writing (essays, stories, and poems) | Literature (genres, reading for understanding and meaning) | Vocabulary (word definitions, pronunciation and spelling) | Formal Speaking and Conversation |
|---|---|---|---|---|---|---|
| **Visual-Spatial** Capacity: forming mental images | Make mental pictures for each part of speech and how to use it correctly in speaking and writing; describe what you're seeing to a partner. | Imagine appropriate locations in which a poem might be read, or mentally see the metaphors, similes, and analogies as pictures. | Create full-blown mental images of something to be written, then write based on those images. | Visualize the settings, characters, action, and anticipated endings of a story. | Create mental pictures to accompany the written definitions of various words you are learning. | Mentally rehearse the speech, including visualizing your audience and their response. |
| **Logical-Mathematical** Capacity: abstract pattern recognition | Identify various grammatical patterns present in various kinds of speaking and writing. | Recognize the distinct linguistic forms of various kinds of poetry and reproduce them. | Use appropriate linguistic forms of various kinds of writing to practice writing on a topic. | Trace plot, character, and setting patterns; patterns of various genres; and patterns within the author's style. | Understand and practice the patterns of various kinds of words in everyday conversation, writing and speaking. | Recognize the patterns of various kinds of public speaking as well as the structural dynamics of an effective speech. |
| **Naturalist** Capacity: sensitivity to flora and fauna | Study influences of nature on language and ways language shapes our relationship with nature, for example the concept of Mother Earth versus Earth as an object to be exploited. | Read poems about nature, then go outdoors and try to re-create the experience of the poetry as fully as you can. | Incorporate analogies from the plant and animal kingdoms into something you are writing or have written. | Examine various pieces of literature and trace the various roles objects and creatures from nature play in them. | Choose a variety of words from a piece of literature and learn the meanings related to the natural world. | Experiment with ways to use the natural world and images to enhance public speaking and informal conversation. |
| **Bodily-Kinesthetic** Capacity: mind-body connections | Experiment with ways certain word combinations evoke bodily responses. | Consciously focus on and feel the physical, bodily impact of various poems, including the impact of associative memories they evoke. | Before writing, spend time exploring the physical connections of the ideas to be communicated, that is, embody them. | Experience visceral bodily responses to events or ideas presented in a literary work. | Study words and memorize their definitions, then create some body movement that connects the various words. | Develop the body language appropriate to communicate your ideas effectively during a formal speech. |

# Year-Long Curriculum Journey for High School
## Focus on English or Foreign Language

| | Grammar (semantics, syntax, and praxis) | Poetry (meters, forms, and figures of speech) | Creative Writing (essays, stories, and poems) | Literature (genres, reading for understanding and meaning) | Vocabulary (word definitions, pronunciation and spelling) | Formal Speaking and Conversation |
|---|---|---|---|---|---|---|
| **Verbal-Linguistic** — Capacity: metalinguistic analysis | Write a sentence and rearrange its words to make a new sentence with a different meaning from that of the first. | Choose a poem about a specific theme and substitute other words for key aspects; read it and see how your substitutions change the meaning. | Rewrite an essay or paragraph by looking up synonyms for as many words as you can find in a thesaurus; note how the meaning changes. | Examine various pieces of literature and read between the lines, looking for possible underlying messages, morals, or themes. | Change the meanings of a sentence through punctuation, word substitutions, or spellings of certain words, such as *night* and *knight*. | Experiment with a variety of ways to communicate a new idea; for example, tailor a speech to very young children, someone from a culture different from yours, and so on. |
| **Auditory-Vibrational** (Musical-Rhythmic) — Capacity: recognizing characteristic qualities of tone | Create tonal rhythmic analogies for each part of speech and how it should be used in writing, for example, an analogy that shows the difference between an action and a state-of-being verb. | Recognize various kinds of poetic meters, rhyming, and free verse poem patterns, and read to re-create a poem's mood. | Create a tonal-rhythmic soundtrack (for example, rhythms, tones, beats, and sound effects) as background accompaniment to your essay or story. | Experiment with sound, rhythms, tones, beats, and vibrations to enhance your experience and increase your comprehension of a literary work. | Recognize the correct pronunciation of words as well as ways the various inflections and emphases affect the meanings. | Use your widest range of tonal and rhythmic patterns to enhance your spoken communication. |
| **Interpersonal** — Capacity: passing into the perspective of another | Explore patterns of speaking, idioms, figures of speech, and so on, from different subcultures in your nation and in other parts of the world. | Understand the life experiences of various poets and ways these experiences shaped and are reflected in their poetry. | Write an essay on a favorite topic from a viewpoint or perspective very different from your own. | Empathize with the various characters in various pieces of literature, villains as well as heroes. | Think of ways someone from a different socio-economic or cultural experience from yours might understand the words. | Practice speaking convincingly from a range of perspectives on a single issue, including those with which you disagree. |
| **Intrapersonal** — Capacity: awareness and expression of various feelings | Understand the range of possible emotions that can be communicated using various parts of speech in speaking and writing. | Note a poem's affective impact on you, including the words, phrases, and images that evoke those feelings. | Practice employing various kinds and styles of writing to evoke various ranges of feelings. | Trace the emotional journeys of characters in a literary work as well as your emotional journey as you read. | Understand the variety of emotive words, phrases, idioms, and so on, noting when and how to use them effectively to produce a desired result. | Create and deliver formal presentations designed to stir the emotions of your audience. |

# Year-Long Curriculum Journey Work Sheet

| | Curriculum Area | Curriculum Area | Curriculum Area | Curriculum Area | Curriculum Area | Curriculum Area |
|---|---|---|---|---|---|---|
| **Visual-Spatial**<br><br>Active imagination<br><br>Finding own way in space<br><br>Forming mental images<br><br>Graphic representation<br><br>Image manipulation<br><br>Recognizing relationships of objects in space<br><br>Accurate perception from various angles | | | | | | |

# Year-Long Curriculum Journey Work Sheet

| | Curriculum Area | Curriculum Area | Curriculum Area | Curriculum Area | Curriculum Area | Curriculum Area |
|---|---|---|---|---|---|---|
| **Bodily-Kinesthetic**<br><br>Control of voluntary movements<br><br>Control of preprogrammed movements<br><br>Expanding awareness through the body<br><br>Mind-body connection<br><br>Mimetic abilities<br><br>Improved body functions | | | | | | |

# Year-Long Curriculum Journey Work Sheet

| | Curriculum Area | Curriculum Area | Curriculum Area | Curriculum Area | Curriculum Area | Curriculum Area |
|---|---|---|---|---|---|---|
| **Logical-Mathematical**<br><br>Abstract pattern recognition<br><br>Inductive reasoning<br><br>Deductive reasoning<br><br>Discerning relationships and connections<br><br>Performing complex calculations<br><br>Scientific reasoning | | | | | | |

# Year-Long Curriculum Journey Work Sheet

| | Curriculum Area | Curriculum Area | Curriculum Area | Curriculum Area | Curriculum Area | Curriculum Area |
|---|---|---|---|---|---|---|
| **Naturalist** | | | | | | |
| Communion with nature | | | | | | |
| Caring for, taming, and interacting with animals | | | | | | |
| Sensitivity to nature's flora | | | | | | |
| Recognizing and classifying species | | | | | | |
| Growing natural things | | | | | | |
| Appreciating the impact of nature | | | | | | |

# Year-Long Curriculum Journey Work Sheet

| | Curriculum Area | Curriculum Area | Curriculum Area | Curriculum Area | Curriculum Area | Curriculum Area |
|---|---|---|---|---|---|---|
| **Verbal-Linguistic**<br><br>Understanding the order and meaning of words<br><br>Convincing someone of a course of action<br><br>Explaining, teaching, and learning<br><br>Linguistic humor<br><br>Memory and recall<br><br>Metalinguistic analysis | | | | | | |

# Year-Long Curriculum Journey Work Sheet

| | Curriculum Area | Curriculum Area | Curriculum Area | Curriculum Area | Curriculum Area | Curriculum Area |
|---|---|---|---|---|---|---|
| **Auditory-Vibrational** (Musical-Rhythmic) | | | | | | |
| Appreciating the structure of music | | | | | | |
| Schemas or frames for hearing music and sound | | | | | | |
| Sensitivity to sound | | | | | | |
| Creating melody, rhythm, and sound | | | | | | |
| Sensing characteristic qualities of tone, sounds, and vibration | | | | | | |

# Year-Long Curriculum Journey Work Sheet

| | Curriculum Area | Curriculum Area | Curriculum Area | Curriculum Area | Curriculum Area | Curriculum Area |
|---|---|---|---|---|---|---|
| **Interpersonal**<br><br>Effective verbal and nonverbal communication<br><br>Noticing and making distinctions between others<br><br>Working cooperatively in a group<br><br>Passing into another's perspective<br><br>Creating and maintaining synergy | | | | | | |

# Year-Long Curriculum Journey Work Sheet

| | Curriculum Area | Curriculum Area | Curriculum Area | Curriculum Area | Curriculum Area | Curriculum Area |
|---|---|---|---|---|---|---|
| **Intrapersonal**<br><br>Concentration of the mind<br><br>Mindfulness<br><br>Metacognition<br><br>Awareness and expression of various feelings<br><br>Transpersonal sense of the self<br><br>Higher-order thinking and reasoning | | | | | | |

# Year-Long Curriculum Journey
# Reflection Log

## Other units I could apply this model to:

## Modifications I would make to this model:

## Things I particularly like about this model:

## The biggest challenges I anticipate in using this model:

# 4
# Unit Stretching

*T*he theory of multiple intelligences helps individual teachers transform existing lessons or units into multimodal learning opportunities for students. Since most teachers are comfortable working with one, two, or perhaps, three intelligences, attempting to integrate additional capacities involves risk-taking and flexibility. The rewards for such efforts are tangible, however. It can be truly satisfying to teach to individual differences. One can observe students' enthusiasm, engagement, and achievement increase and experience the expansion of one's own intellectual capacities.

—Linda Campbell, Bruce Campbell, and Dee Dickinson
*Teaching and Learning through Multiple Intelligences* (173)

The idea for the Unit Stretching model comes from a high school history teacher in Miami, Florida. After extensive training in the theory of multiple intelligences, this teacher decided that he needed to use this information as he designed and executed the various units that comprised the history curriculum for which he was responsible.

## Purpose of the Unit Stretching Model

The fundamental intent of the Unit Stretching model is to inventory the MI capacities that are part of plans for an existing unit of study or for a theme by passing it through a multiple intelligence analytic screen such as the MI Capacities Wheels.

## Goals of the Unit Stretching Model

■ To recognize the "intelligence capacities" that are already being addressed in the unit, whether or not you had the language of MI to analyze the unit at the time it was designed

■ To note the intelligence areas that are not used fully (given the capacities) in the unit, and those that have been avoided or that are represented only in a fairly superficial manner

■ To stretch the unit to incorporate the capacities of the weak and/or neglected intelligence areas in the teaching of the unit's content

## The Development of the Unit Stretching Model

Before starting a new unit, the history teacher spent some planning time analyzing the unit using the MI Capacities Wheels (pages 19 and 20). Looking at a unit he had taught in the past, he used the capacities wheels to inventory the capacities that were already part of the unit. Next he analyzed the unit to determine which intelligences were left out or which were weakly represented. He then used the capacities wheels to incorporate additional capacities to beef up the intelligences, so to speak, that were weakly represented.

The particular unit he shared with me was one dealing with Europe during the Middle Ages. As he inventoried the unit using the capacities wheels, he realized that the auditory-vibrational (musical-rhythmic) intelligence was weakly represented. He invited the high school voice instructor to come into his history classes and teach students how to do Gregorian chant (number one on the pop music charts for this historical era!).

Notice what he made happen in this unit: *students are learning music in history class!* He basically stretched the parameters of his unit.

On a later day, he asked students to create their own chants, using the Gregorian form, but their subject matter was to be something that concerned them as teenagers living in the latter days of the twentieth century. Again, notice what happened to this unit: *students are now composing music in history!* He shared with me an astonishing array of chants that dealt with such varied topics as fear of AIDS, ways to say no to drugs, dates for the prom, domestic violence, worries about making it into the college or university of their choice, being accepted by their peers, and so on—all topics of concern to today's young people.

## Things about This Model That Excite and Interest Me

■ *It recognizes that we are already incorporating multiple intelligences into our units to some degree, often without calling it MI.* In some ways, there is nothing new about the theory of multiple intelligences. We have always known that we are all different, that these differences are important, they are fun, they are exciting, and they are to be honored and celebrated. Also, in some ways teaching with multiple intelligences has always been the definition of good teaching, even when we didn't have an MI label to define what we were doing. Good teachers have always known that they must vary instruction and provide a wide variety of learning experiences for students if all students are to deeply understand various concepts.

What *is* new is that we now have an immense body of research from the frontiers of contemporary brain-mind research, cognitive sciences, psychology, and twentieth-century educational research that validates what we have always intuitively known: individual students are unique and unrepeatable creatures, and we must take their unique natures very seriously when we seek to educate them.

■ *It proves that it is possible to take a good plan, expand it, and make it better.* Once we have become conscious of the various MI strategies we have been using, perhaps unconsciously or intuitively, we can continue what we have been doing with greater understanding of why it works, we can do it more frequently, more intentionally, more strategically, and more precisely. Such professional growth raises the level of the teaching profession to new heights.

Of course, one challenge we face is to make sure that the general public, including parents, grows with us. Given what research reveals are state-of-the-art, best teaching and learning practices, we can no longer tolerate the simplistic "back to basics" agenda for school renewal and reform, nor can we afford to allow "how it was when I went to school" to dominate policy in our schools. Today we know more than humankind has ever known about the human brain, about what it takes to help students transfer learning from the classroom to everyday life, about how to provide high-level, challenging, creative educational experiences to *all* students, not just those who have been identified as gifted and talented by a variety of linguistically and logically biased assessment tools. We know that schooling must fit the learner rather than insisting that the learner fit it. We know that instruction is more a matter of facilitation and coaching than the stand and deliver, sage on the stage approach (thanks to Roger Taylor for this image!).

■ *It necessitates the effective use of other faculty members' strengths and gifts.* We all have eight intelligences, probably more! They are part of our biology and neurology as human beings. However, not all of our intelligences are equally developed. Some of them may even be asleep. Some may be on vacation. But they are all potentially able to be awakened! The history teacher who developed this model recognized the importance of incorporating auditory-vibrational capacities into the unit, but he also recognized the need for an outside consultant (the voice instructor) who was strong in this intelligence. After students learned the music form, he, *on his own*, built on that knowledge throughout the unit and provided opportunities for students to further develop their auditory-vibrational capacities.

Within this Unit Stretching model are multiple opportunities for creating a profound collegiality among school staff, grade level interdisciplinary teams, or within a curriculum-based department. In this approach, teachers *must* rely on one another's talents, gifts, creativity, and strengths in the various intelligences to design effective units. Once you have built the consensus that all the MI capacities need to be addressed in and through the curriculum as often as possible, then it is almost a fait accompli that you will help one another and share expertise in the various intelligences. In many instances in my work with schools and school districts in the United States and school divisions in Canada, I have witnessed an incredible camaraderie result from the commitment to stretch units in this way.

## The Basic Process

Following are steps for utilizing the Unit Stretching work sheet (please refer to the examples on pages 92–108.

**Step 1** Outline the basic content for the unit in as much detail as possible so that you are clear on all of its dynamics. Don't rely on your memory or on what you think you have done. As fully as possible, re-create the most recent version of the unit. Only such attention will give you a full opportunity to stretch the unit.

**Step 2** Articulate your instructional objectives and outcomes for the unit: What do you want students to know and understand at the end of the unit? What skills do you want them to acquire, practice, or develop? This step is extremely important to ensure that you maintain the academic integrity of the unit.

Without a clear focus on the objective or outcome, you can easily render a unit an interesting string of fun, creative activities that are only tangentially related to the intent of the curriculum. A clear articulation of objectives helps you focus every part of the teaching and learning process on helping students master the content *and* develop their MI capacities.

**Step 3**  Use the MI Capacities Wheels on pages 19 and 20 to inventory the intelligence capacities in the unit. Your intent is first to note the specific capacities that are already part of the unit. It helps to connect as much as possible every part of the unit to one of the capacities on the wheel. You may find it useful for your own clarity to briefly describe the connections you see between the unit and the MI capacities. Then list those connections in the first blank column of the work sheet. For example, in your existing unit, you may already have students *role-playing* certain concepts (bodily-kinesthetic **mimetic ability**) or *visualizing* (visual-spatial ability to **form mental images**) or *working in cooperative groups* (interpersonal ability to **work cooperatively on a team**). Use the capacities wheels to help you pinpoint these capacities.

**Step 4**  Note any intelligences that are weakly represented for whatever reason, either absent entirely or only superficial. Be as objective and honest with yourself as possible as you conduct this analysis. Do not be hard on or critical of yourself over the weak or avoided areas; the whole purpose of this model is to assist you in stretching your conceptualization of the unit to make it more effective. Harsh judgment and criticism really have no place in this endeavor because they can often get in the way of genuine professional development and human transformation.

**Step 5**  In the last blank column, under "New Opportunities," list specific capacities that you will incorporate into the old plan to stretch underutilized or avoided intelligences. Include a brief description of the learning activities you will do to incorporate these capacities. This exercise requires high-level creativity, so don't rush it. Give your ideas a chance to incubate. Write down an idea, then leave it alone for a couple of days. Let it age, like a fine wine, then taste it again and see if it still seems to be on target.

**Step 6**  Record the capacities you have used in this unit so that you can incorporate others in future units. Be careful not to overuse certain capacities just because you find them easier or more comfortable. One intent of the Unit Stretching model is to help you utilize all the capacities at least once during a given term. Many teachers have told me that as they work with stretching their units, the task of embedding the capacities in units becomes easier and easier. While I am not strongly advocating it, you may even find that eventually you will be able to incorporate all the capacities of all the intelligences into a single unit!

## Evaluations of the Model

Following are some of my own thoughts about the pluses and minuses of the Unit Stretching model. I hope you and your colleagues will engage in a similar evaluation of this model in your department, school, or district to find the approach that is best suited to your situation. Some of what I mention here is stated earlier, but I want to reiterate it:

### + + + PLUSES + + +

▶ **It builds on work already done.** This approach uses units that have already been thought through; you are not starting at ground zero. In other words, you don't have to reinvent the wheel!

▶ **It expands unit conceptualization.** This approach requires you to think about new ways the unit concepts can be taught. It suggests that all concepts can be covered in new, interesting ways that engage students' full range of intelligence capacities. It asks you to push the edges of your own creativity and to explore the unit from new vantage points, seeing how many ways you can create to develop the concepts of a given unit.

▶ **It enriches a teacher's understanding of a unit.** Many teachers have told me that when they decided to stretch a unit in the ways suggested, they learned many new things about the concepts themselves! The reason may be that knowing is amplified when we use all of our intelligences. We know our content on many more levels of our brain-mind-body system than we have in the past.

▶ **It keeps you fresh and creative.** Can you remember the first time you taught this unit? Can you recall the anticipation and maybe even a bit of the nervousness about whether your plan would work? This approach helps you recover some of the initial excitement, even when you're teaching concepts that you have probably taught hundreds of times over the years!

▶ **It amplifies the learning process.** This approach provides students with opportunities to gain a deep understanding of the material that goes beyond mere head knowledge. It requires them not only to represent the various concepts involved in the unit in multiple ways, but it also helps them to transfer and integrate the learning in profound ways. Current brain and educational research documents that, when learning occurs via multiple modalities, not only does it tend to stick, but the multimodal, multisensory approach itself promotes dendritic growth.

## – – – MINUSES – – –

▶ **It requires some trial and error.** While I believe that in principle all the capacities could be included within a given unit, it takes a fair amount of experimentation and a willingness to try some new approaches to figure out which capacities are most appropriate given the unit's content. One danger is that we trivialize or in some way pervert the integrity of the concepts being taught just to be able to say "I used all the intelligences!" You can quite easily guard against such a trap, however. The key is to focus your work with the capacities very clearly on your ultimate objectives and outcomes for the unit. Bear in mind that it is not imperative for you to use all the capacities, or even all intelligences, in a unit; the goal is to incorporate all the capacities into the most appropriate places throughout the curriculum, perhaps one unit at a time.

▶ **It may meet with student resistance.** Some students may initially feel uncomfortable when asked to use certain capacities. However, if you take some time to teach them about the intelligences, to validate all eight ways of knowing, and to help them learn ways to use each one effectively to enhance their own learning, you will find that they get used to the idea and even grow with it. Initially this task may seem like an add-on, but it is well worth the time.

▶ **You may have assessment anxiety.** District or school division and state or provincial tests, for the most part, have not yet made the transition to truly multimodal assessments. Although most of us hate and are opposed to these tests, we nevertheless must administer them, and our performance evaluations are often directly linked to students' performance on them. You may fear trying something new that may not result in higher test scores. However, remember that an MI approach leads to deeper, more thorough understanding, and you may find that students who never did well on such tests perform better because you are helping them understand the concepts as well as those who seem to do well.

▶ **It is time consuming.** While this approach is an extremely *effective* way to teach a unit in terms of students' in-depth understanding, it is not an *efficient* way to cover a certain amount of material by a certain date. Use of this model forces you to make some important curricular decisions regarding which units or parts of units warrant this time and effort. Begin by using the units that most readily lend themselves to this kind of scrutiny and reworking, then figure out your own strategies for meeting "coverage" deadlines.

# Elementary

## Reading and Understanding a Story

In this unit, students read and discuss a story. The unit focuses on developing reading comprehension, understanding key components or aspects that are part of any good piece of literature, vocabulary development, characterization, and personal learnings and identifications with the story.

## Academic Objectives and Outcomes

- To increase students' reading comprehension, including their understanding of the plot, characters, and setting

- To learn and understand new vocabulary words, idioms, and other figures of speech that are used in the story and how to use them in daily speech and communication with others

- To understand the classic parts of a story (plot, setting, characters) and the dynamic role of each part in the story

- To analyze and understand the various characters in the story, including personality characteristics, motivations, worldviews and perspectives on life, feelings and emotional responses, dynamic relationships to and effect on other characters

- To explore personal connections and identifications with the story, including values, life goals, self-discoveries, learning and discoveries about others, and pitfalls to avoid or really smart things to do

Choose a reading unit that generally spans three to four weeks. You might use a single story with younger children or a whole book with older ones. Begin by analyzing the unit using the MI Capacities Wheels on pages 19 and 20. In the first column of the chart on pages 93–94 list the learning tasks that are already part of the unit as you have conducted it in the past. You will probably discover that you have already, knowingly or by "accident", hit on some of the capacities and they are already part of the unit. Try to link these things with the intelligence capacities in the center column. Once you have inventoried the unit as taught in the past, I suggest that you focus on those specific intelligence areas where the unit needs stretching. In the last column select at least one additional capacity to include in the unit, and maybe more than one at those points where you feel the unit could really use some "intelligence beefing up"!

The example (pages 92–94) illustrates ways to incorporate a few practical suggestions for each intelligence to stretch students' experience. Please study the example before beginning.

## Commentary on the Elementary
## Unit Stretching Model Example

Obviously, reading and reading comprehension are keys to success in any nation of our globe and in any career path one chooses to follow. Using MI teaching and learning strategies in reading is a powerful way not only to improve reading skills in their own right, but more important, to help students comprehend what they have read. As I have tried to illustrate, there are many other aspects of developing skill in the language arts that benefit from incorporating all of the intelligences.

Following are some of my reflections, thoughts, insights, and other metacognitive postscripts and ramblings on this example.

- As you consider the example, remember that my goal is to demonstrate ways to use this model with standard elementary reading material. I present a generic example that could work equally well with a basal reader, whole language approach, and a wealth of children's literature.

- Play with this unit so it becomes your own. There is really no way simply to use the unit as is. The example is more or less without content. You must pour the specific content of the reading you want children to do into the framework I have provided.

- I chose the capacities in this example for very utilitarian reasons; namely, they fit most obviously with the implied content. However, in principle, I could have highlighted any of the capacities. Once you are into the unit, so to speak, make your own empirical judgments about which capacities are best suited to the content at hand, but *be careful that your own biases or comfort zones don't get in the way of the creative possibilities for stretching the unit.*

- While the various capacities (or "core operations") of the intelligences are fairly precise (see chapter 2), *how* they are incorporated into a unit must be in line with your objectives and outcomes, and they must be tweaked to fit appropriately with the content. However, I also feel that it is important, as much as possible, to maintain the cognitive integrity of the intelligence. That is, you must couch the learning and instruction within the unique cognitive operation of the intelligence with which you are working. For example, if you stretch the unit so students are working with the visual-spatial capacity *graphic representation,* you must allow students to use the actual media of the intelligence (paints, clay, montage, chalk, colored markers, collage) so the intelligence gets exercised *and* you achieve the objectives or outcomes of the unit!

■ Although, as I mention in the previous point, that it's important to honor the precise cognitive modality of the intelligences, note that in reality and in normal people, you will never see an intelligence in isolation. The intelligences and their related capacities tend to operate as integrated, well-orchestrated wholes, although certain individual tendencies may utilize certain intelligences and even certain capacities within an intelligence more than others. While you are stretching a unit, you will always be stretching some students, while others will feel very much "at home." However, within the overall design of the unit you will be dealing with all of the intelligences, thus dealing with all of the tendencies of all of your students in and through the unit, as well as providing opportunities and expectations that all students will stretch and try some new things.

# Unit Stretching in Elementary School

## Reading and Understanding a Story

### Objectives and Outcomes
What are the key concepts and skills you want to address?

Students will be able to read a story and identify the key parts (see page 89 for more detail).

### Room Arrangements
What various spaces for groups and individuals do you require?

- plan for a story setting field trip
- reading group centers with various stories
- art center
- acting center

### Resources
What materials, equipment, supplies, speakers, videos, and so on do you need?

- a variety of children's storybooks
- art supplies, including paints, marking pens, and colored chalk
- dress-up clothes and costumes
- audiocassette recorder
- instruments for making sounds or music (students can create these, as well)

### Assessment
What multimodal projects will you require of students to evaluate their learning?

Using at least three intelligences, students demonstrate the key parts of a story, including an understanding of the role and function of each part.

# Unit Stretching in Elementary School
## Reading and Understanding a Story

| | Already Teach (MI capacities already part of the unit plan) | Multiple Intelligences Capacities Inventory | New Opportunities (additional MI capacities to be included in the plan) |
|---|---|---|---|
| **Visual-Spatial Intelligence** | | ▼ Active imagination<br>▼ Forming mental images<br>▼ Finding own way in space<br>▼ Graphic representation<br>▼ Recognition of relationships between objects in space<br>▼ Image manipulation<br>▼ Accurate perception from various angles | ■ Active imagination: Create scribbles, then find things in it that are related to the story.<br>■ Forming mental images: Visualize characters, action, and settings in the story.<br>■ Graphic representation: Draw or paint pictures of the settings, characters, action scenes, and plot. |
| **Logical-Mathematical Intelligence** | | ▼ Abstract pattern recognition<br>▼ Inductive reasoning<br>▼ Deductive reasoning<br>▼ Discerning relationships and connections<br>▼ Performing complex calculations<br>▼ Scientific thinking | ■ Graphic organizers: Use Venn diagrams, webs, and so on, to understand characters.<br>■ Inductive reasoning: Anticipate and predict outcomes based on facts in a story.<br>■ Abstract pattern recognition: Learn to recognize key parts of the story that are part of any story. |
| **Bodily-Kinesthetic Intelligence** | | ▼ Voluntary body movements<br>▼ Preprogrammed body movements<br>▼ Expanding awareness through the body<br>▼ Mind-body connections<br>▼ Mimetic abilities<br>▼ Improved body functions | ■ Mimetic abilities: Become a character in the story for a day; that is, dress in costume, use speech and actions.<br>■ Improved body functions: Learn how to do something a character in the story does but that you can't yet.<br>■ Mind-body connections: Get inside the mind and body of the character (for example, understand moods, posture, walk, facial expressions, and so on). |
| **Naturalist Intelligence** | | ▼ Communion with nature<br>▼ Sensitivity to nature's flora<br>▼ Ability to care for, tame, and interact with living creatures<br>▼ Appreciating nature's impact<br>▼ Species classification | ■ Communion with nature: Imagine yourself in the story's natural settings and note how they affect you.<br>■ Species classification: Study any animal and plant groupings in the story.<br>■ Appreciating nature's impact: Go outdoors and experience natural setting of the story. |

# Unit Stretching in Elementary School
## Reading and Understanding a Story

| | **Already Teach** (MI capacities already part of the unit plan) | **Multiple Intelligences Capacities Inventory** | **New Opportunities** (additional MI capacities to be included in the plan) |
|---|---|---|---|
| **Verbal-Linguistic Intelligence** | | ▼ Understanding the order and meaning of words<br>▼ Explaining, teaching, and learning<br>▼ Linguistic humor<br>▼ Convincing someone to take a course of action<br>▼ Memory and recall<br>▼ Metalinguistic analysis | ■ Understanding order and meanings of words: Learn the vocabulary, idioms, and so on in the story.<br>■ Metalinguistic analysis: Study the nuances of the dialogue between characters.<br>■ Convince someone of a course of action: Become a character in the story and make persuasive statements about a concern in character. |
| **Auditory-Vibrational Intelligence** (Musical-Rhythmic) | | ▼ Appreciation for the structure of music and rhythm<br>▼ Schemas or frames for hearing music and rhythm<br>▼ Sensitivity to sound<br>▼ Recognition, creation, and reproduction of melody, rhythm, and sound<br>▼ Recognizing characteristic qualities of tones and rhythm | ■ Schemas or frames for hearing music: Create a soundtrack for the story and what your life would be like as an additional character.<br>■ Recognition, creation, reproduction of melody, rhythm, and sound: Retell the story by making up songs about the characters, plot, action, and outcome.<br>■ Appreciation for the structure of music and rhythm: Create a musical and rhythm theme for each character and setting, such as that in *Peter and the Wolf*. |
| **Interpersonal Intelligence** | | ▼ Effective verbal and nonverbal communication<br>▼ Accurately reading others' moods, temperaments, motivations, and feelings<br>▼ Working cooperatively in a group<br>▼ Listening to and appreciating another's perspective<br>▼ Passing into the life of another<br>▼ Creating and maintaining synergy | ■ Passing into the life of another: Imagine being in the story and what your life would be like as an additional character.<br>■ Listening to and appreciating another's perspective: Understand why various characters act in the way they do based on their perspective on life.<br>■ Working cooperatively in a group: Work together in reading teams to understand the story and to perform the various learning activities related to the story. |
| **Intrapersonal Intelligence** | | ▼ Concentration<br>▼ Mindfulness<br>▼ Metacognition<br>▼ Awareness and expression of various feelings<br>▼ Transpersonal sense of the self<br>▼ Higher-order thinking and reasoning | ■ Higher-order reasoning: Reflect on personal identifications with various situations or parts of the story.<br>■ Metacognition: Think about and analyze the thought patterns of the various characters as if they were you and say how you would change the thinking.<br>■ Transpersonal sense of self: Retell the story with yourself as one of the characters.<br>■ Awareness of feelings: Think about and share personal feelings about the story. |

# Middle School

## A Health-Conscious Diet

In this unit, students study the major food groups and learn how to apply this information to creating a healthy, balanced diet. The unit focuses not only on understanding the foods we eat and their effects on the body, but also on helping students seriously evaluate their own eating habits to establish a healthier lifestyle.

## Academic Objectives and Outcomes

- To understand the major food groups, which foods are members of each group, the recommended daily amount for each, and ways to recognize this amount when, for example, dining out at a restaurant or at someone's house

- To learn *why* the body needs the major food groups in certain quantities each day and how to apply this information to plan healthy, nutritionally balanced, and exciting menus

- To analyze own eating patterns in light of what comprises a healthy diet and to set realistic goals for establishing more healthy, balanced eating practices

- To learn exciting food preparation techniques that maintain food's nutritional value

- To experiment with alternative, healthy ways of enhancing the flavor of food, such as using herbs, sodium substitutes, low-calorie and low-fat dressings, and so on

In my example, I am more or less "starting from scratch" on planning a health unit that meets the objectives. You, however, should work with a unit that takes four to five weeks. For purposes of comparison, select a unit that has similar, although not necessarily identical, content as my example. Begin by analyzing the unit using the MI Capacities Wheels on pages 19 and 20. In the first column of the work sheet, list the learning tasks that are already part of the unit as you have conducted it in the past. Link these activities with the MI capacities in the center column. You may find some of my stretching suggestions are already part of your unit. Initially, focus on those specific intelligences that are weakly or superficially represented; work your "stretching magic" there. Include these ideas in the last column of the chart.

My example (pages 99–101) illustrates suggestions of ways to stretch students' learning about healthy foods, nutrition, and eating by incorporating a few capacities for each intelligence into the unit. Please study the example before beginning.

## Commentary on the Middle School
## Unit Stretching Model Example

The typical middle school health curriculum deals with a number of important concepts that are foundational to establishing lifelong patterns of health. Unfortunately, other than the aspects that deal with human sexuality, most students find this curriculum rather tedious, especially when it implies changing their existing lifestyle. An MI approach to this curriculum can very quickly engage both students and teacher.

Following are some of my reflections, thoughts, insights, and other "metacognitive postscripts" on the example:

- As you peruse the example, remember that I am not making curricular content recommendations; that is, I am not suggesting that this particular content be included in your health curriculum. My goal is to demonstrate how to use the Unit Stretching model with a unit of what could be typical middle school material.

- The example illustrates certain aspects of what some of the educational literature today is calling a *constructivist approach* to the curriculum, although not in the strictest sense. The process of the unit takes a certain body of knowledge and provides students with an opportunity to construct connections to their own lives, to create meaning for themselves, and to discover personal implications and applications of the various concepts. The unit and its various learning tasks are set up to lead students to discover the importance of the curriculum concepts in their own lives. As they use the various intelligences to study the material, it suddenly becomes more than just "head knowledge" or "book knowledge." They know it in and through their bodies, through their seeing, through their relating to others, through their senses of taste and smell, and so on.

- I chose the specific capacities to incorporate into the example because I felt they were clearly the most on target, given the stated desired objectives and outcomes for the unit. I am not suggesting that others could not have been included, as well. In fact, I would be the first to make the case that, in principle, all the capacities of all of the intelligences *could* be incorporated into the unit. Nevertheless, the desired objectives and outcomes of the unit must dictate the specific capacities you include.

■ Philosophically, my first goal is to achieve balance among the intelligence capacities employed in a unit; and, second, to ensure that during a specified period of time, such as a term, you highlight all of the capacities of all the intelligences. A helpful discipline in this regard is to keep a careful log of the capacities you have incorporated into a given unit, then look to use a different set of capacities in the next unit.

■ Students need opportunities to work with specific capacities over a period of time not only to build their confidence in using the full range of their intellectual capacities, but also to increase their skill. This task is very much like that involved in the development of any skill—practice makes perfect! So while I believe that working with all the capacities is important, you must balance that approach with allowing students to more fully develop and enhance their skills in selected capacities, as well.

# Unit Stretching in Middle School
## A Healthy Diet

## Objectives and Outcomes
What are the key concepts and skills you want to address?

Students will understand the steps involved in planning and implementing a healthy diet.

## Room Arrangements
What various spaces for groups and individuals do you require?

- space for an herb garden
- a food preparation center
- a food sampling area

## Resources
What materials, equipment, supplies, speakers, videos, and so on do you need?

- magazines with pictures of various foods
- a collection of food labels from boxes, cans, and bottles
- audiocassette or CD player and various kinds of music

## Assessment
What multimodal projects will you require of students to evaluate their learning?

Students create a poster that illustrates a month's plan for implementing a healthy diet. The plan must include explanations of each part to demonstrate understanding of various concepts.

# Unit Stretching in Middle School
## A Healthy Diet

| | Already Teach (MI capacities already part of the unit plan) | Multiple Intelligences Capacities Inventory | New Opportunities (additional MI capacities to be included in the plan) |
|---|---|---|---|
| Visual-Spatial Intelligence | | ▼ Active imagination<br>▼ Forming mental images<br>▼ Finding own way in space<br>▼ Graphic representation<br>▼ Recognition of relationships between objects in space<br>▼ Image manipulation<br>▼ Accurate perception from various angles | ■ Forming mental images: Visualize eating a healthy, balanced diet every day for one month and the results you will see.<br>■ Graphic representation: Make montages, posters, collages, that illustrate the major food groups.<br>■ Finding your way in space: Imagine a local grocery store and note where the healthy items are located. |
| Logical-Mathematical Intelligence | | ▼ Abstract pattern recognition<br>▼ Inductive reasoning<br>▼ Deductive reasoning<br>▼ Discerning relationships and connections<br>▼ Performing complex calculations<br>▼ Scientific thinking | ■ Performing complex calculations: Learn how to read and understand food labels and how to use the information to plan a healthy diet.<br>■ Discerning relationships and connections: Figure out ways to adjust your food intake based on what you have already consumed today.<br>■ Abstract pattern recognition: Apply the major food group schema to your daily eating patterns. |
| Bodily-Kinesthetic Intelligence | | ▼ Voluntary body movements<br>▼ Preprogrammed body movements<br>▼ Expanding awareness through the body<br>▼ Mind-body connections<br>▼ Mimetic abilities<br>▼ Improved body functions | ■ Mind-body connections: Experiment with the effects of various foods and substances (caffeine, sugar, fiber, and so on) on your mind and body.<br>■ Preprogrammed body movements: Practice reprogramming your body to crave healthy foods.<br>■ Improved body functions: For a month, eat only healthy foods; do a before and after analysis of the results. |
| Naturalist Intelligence | | ▼ Communion with nature<br>▼ Sensitivity to nature's flora<br>▼ Ability to care for, tame, and interact with living creatures<br>▼ Appreciating nature's impact<br>▼ Species classification | ■ Growing things: Plant an herb garden and learn ways to use herbs to season while cooking and eating.<br>■ Communion with nature: Study ways nature and the environment affect your dining experience.<br>■ Species classification: Learn ways to recognize the food groups in a meal; analyze the meal for proper balance. |

# Unit Stretching in Middle School
## A Healthy Diet

| | Already Teach (MI capacities already part of the unit plan) | Multiple Intelligences Capacities Inventory | New Opportunities (additional MI capacities to be included in the plan) |
|---|---|---|---|
| **Verbal-Linguistic Intelligence** | | ▼ Understanding the order and meaning of words<br>▼ Explaining, teaching, and learning<br>▼ Linguistic humor<br>▼ Convincing someone to take a course of action<br>▼ Memory and recall<br>▼ Metalinguistic analysis | ■ Explaining, teaching, and learning: Study a recipe and explain to someone else ways to substitute healthy ingredients for those that are not healthy.<br>■ Convincing someone of a course of action: Write a speech or an essay that details why one should follow a healthy diet.<br>■ Linguistic humor: Make up a series of limericks, jokes, puns, and so on, about the major food groups. |
| **Auditory-Vibrational Intelligence** (musical-rhythmic) | | ▼ Recognizing characteristic qualities of tones and rhythm<br>▼ Recognition, creation, and reproduction of melody, rhythm, and sound<br>▼ Sensitivity to sound<br>▼ Schemas or frames for hearing music and rhythm<br>▼ Appreciation for the structure of music and rhythm | ■ Appreciation for the structure of music and rhythm: Research the impact of various kinds of music on the dining experience and on digestion.<br>■ Recognizing characteristic qualities of tones and rhythm. Create a game based on the sounds of various foods being eaten, such as biting into a juicy apple.<br>■ Schemas or frames for hearing music and rhythm: Compare and contrast sounds various students make while eating various kinds of food, such as chocolate, raw broccoli. |
| **Interpersonal Intelligence** | | ▼ Effective verbal and nonverbal communication<br>▼ Accurately reading others' moods, temperaments, motivations, and feelings<br>▼ Working cooperatively in a group<br>▼ Understanding from another's perspective<br>▼ Passing into the life of another<br>▼ Creating and maintaining synergy | ■ Accurately reading others' moods, temperaments, motivations, and feelings: Discern a person's response to a meal or a food by observing them.<br>■ Effective verbal and nonverbal communication: Keep a log of conversations you have during meal times; note the similarities and differences between them and conversations that happen when no food is present.<br>■ Listening to and appreciating another's perspective: Discuss a hated food with someone who loves it; explain why that person loves it. |
| **Intrapersonal Intelligence** | | ▼ Concentration<br>▼ Mindfulness<br>▼ Metacognition<br>▼ Awareness and expression of various feelings<br>▼ Transpersonal sense of the self<br>▼ Higher-order thinking and reasoning | ■ Mindfulness: Play an awareness game while eating: notice everything that occurs in the brain-mind-body system; note ways you can alter your responses to food.<br>■ Concentration of the mind: Eat something very, very slowly; see how long you can continue to taste it after you have swallowed.<br>■ Higher-order thinking and reasoning: Using a model of the major food groups, plan a month's worth of interesting and exciting meals that are wholly balanced. |

# High School

## The Journey to Employment

This unit is in the business department. Students learn what is involved in getting and keeping a job. The unit starts at ground zero with setting employment goals, learning how to create a winning resume, filling out job applications, interviewing, and so on. During the course of the unit are several simulations that give student opportunities to apply their learning.

## Academic Objectives and Outcomes

- To articulate employment goals and to match these goals with potential jobs that provide the training and experience to reach the next goal

- To learn how to use life experiences to create a successful resume; includes structure and form of a resume, appropriate language to use, and ways to adjust the resume for various potential employers

- To learn how to fill out employment applications and obtain an interview

- To understand the protocol of a job interview, including appropriate dress and behavior, and ways to direct the interview to cover certain points regarding qualifications

- To learn ways to evaluate the relative success of the interview at its conclusion and to plan strategies for following up the interview

The example assumes a class of students who are learning various skills needed on the job, including people skills and some of the more practical skills. While this specific content may not be a whole unit in your curriculum, choose a unit to work with that has some similarities. Begin by analyzing the unit using the MI Capacities Wheels on pages 19 and 20. In the first column of the charts on pages 107–8 list the learning tasks and MI capacities that are already part of the unit as you have conducted it in the past. Match these as closely as you can with the capacities for the different intelligences in the center column. You will most certainly find that some of these capacities are already part of the unit. Note where the unit needs strengthening in terms of the relative balance of the intelligences. I suggest that you initially focus the stretching on these points of the unit. In the last column, select additional capacities to include, both (and especially) those weak or underdeveloped points you noted when analyzing the unit with the MI Capacities Wheel, and other capacities you feel could enhance students' learning of the material and experience of the unit.

My example (pages 106–8) illustrates practical suggestions of ways to stretch students' experience of the unit by incorporating a few suggestions for each intelligence. Please study the example before beginning.

## Commentary on the High School Unit Stretching Model Example

This unit deals with the development of an extremely important life skill: how to find and keep a job. I demonstrate ways to take this beyond the mechanics of such things as filling out a job application to a realistic, authentic simulation of the entire process, from first interest in a certain job to the preparation process, including writing a resume, filling out an application, and interviewing.

Following are some of my reflections, thoughts, insights, and other "metacognitive postscripts" on this example:

- When dealing with content that relies heavily on particular intelligences (in this case, verbal-linguistic and interpersonal), there are a couple of interesting directions you can take with the stretching strategies. You can focus on the intelligences that are inherent in the content. Using the unit in this example, you would stretch the unit to incorporate *all* of the capacities of verbal-linguistic and interpersonal intelligences. You can decide instead to focus on stretching the unit to incorporate the intelligences that are not naturally included. I took this approach in this example, stretching to include capacities from all the intelligences, not just the obvious ones.

- One of the dangers of the Unit Stretching model, especially at the secondary level, is that you lose focus on the content by trying to incorporate too many capacities in a learning task. Once you have figured out all the ways to stretch the unit, further stretch it by distributing the capacities over time, making sure that your academic objectives are clear. Include the content focus in the description of the stretching activities. I illustrate this technique in my descriptions.

- As with the example unit for the elementary and middle school levels, the high school example should not be perceived as a suggested piece of content for the business department, or any other for that matter. The only curricular value of the example is to illustrate the Unit Stretching model with typical secondary content.

One thing this unit illustrates is what some of the literature is calling *in-context learning*. Much of what we teach in secondary education is somewhat remote from the daily lives of most high school students. In-context learning places learning in the context of life beyond school. If we cannot say why a student needs algebra, English literature, or any other content, I question whether it should be part of the curriculum. I often wonder how much is in the curriculum for purely sentimental reasons, that is, because it's always been part of school, so it must be right. A second fallacy is insisting it be important to students because it is important to us (teachers, parents, the larger community, even the nation). Such an attitude doesn't make it more important to students; they must see the connections to their own lives. Once we have established in our own minds what students really need to live effectively, now and in their adult lives, we should teach those concepts in ways that make their importance apparent to students. For the purposes of illustrating how to use this model, I chose content whose meaningful transfer to life is fairly obvious. When you are working with content whose transfer is less obvious, use the capacities in ways that help students discover the relevance of the material for their own lives today and in the future.

The Unit Stretching model is the easiest to implement at the high school level; generally teachers already have a large archive of fully developed lessons for the various parts of the department's curriculum. This model asks you to build on this fine work and expand students' learning experience. Many teachers who have used this model have told me that in the process of stretching units, they learned new things about the very content they had been teaching for many years! This model asks you to look at what you've always taught with brand new eyes, or from a novel and unexpected perspective. However, remember there is a big difference between distorting the content to make it fit the MI capacities and stretching it to allow students a more holistic encounter with the material.

# Unit Stretching in High School

## Journey to Employment

### Objectives and Outcomes
What are the key concepts and skills you want to address?

Students will understand the steps involved in procuring a job and will know how to create a resume, fill out job applications, and take part in successful interviews.

### Room Arrangements
What various spaces for groups and individuals do you require?

- spaces for students to meet in cooperative learning groups
- spaces for students to do individual work
- a furniture arrangement for conducting simulated job interviews

### Resources
What materials, equipment, supplies, speakers, videos, and so on do you need?

- sample resumes
- a variety of job applications for practice
- newspaper want ads
- audiocassette or CD players and a variety of music

### Assessment
What multimodal projects will you require of students to evaluate their learning?

Students turn in three completed job applications with appropriate resumes, a videotape of a mock job interview conducted by another student, and a time line that shows personal employment goals and a plan to achieve them.

# Unit Stretching in High School
## Journey to Employment

| | Already Teach (MI capacities already part of the unit plan) | Multiple Intelligences Capacities Inventory | New Opportunities (additional MI capacities to be included in the plan) |
|---|---|---|---|
| **Visual-Spatial Intelligence** | | ▼ Active imagination<br>▼ Forming mental images<br>▼ Finding own way in space<br>▼ Graphic representation<br>▼ Recognition of relationships between objects in space<br>▼ Image manipulation<br>▼ Accurate perception from various angles | ■ Forming mental images: Visualize an entire interview, mentally practicing responses to potential questions.<br>■ Recognizing relationships between objects in space: Learn to observe and respond to the spatial components of a potential job.<br>■ Image manipulation: Practice seeing a job-related situation from a point of view different from your own. |
| **Logical-Mathematical Intelligence** | | ▼ Abstract pattern recognition<br>▼ Inductive reasoning<br>▼ Deductive reasoning<br>▼ Discerning relationships and connections<br>▼ Performing complex calculations<br>▼ Scientific thinking | ■ Deductive reasoning: Set employment goals, then brainstorm the steps needed to achieve the goal.<br>■ Inductive reasoning: Learn ways to use your past experience to create a convincing resume.<br>■ Scientific thinking: Practice making connections between your own employment goals and potential jobs. |
| **Bodily-Kinesthetic Intelligence** | | ▼ Voluntary body movements<br>▼ Preprogrammed body movements<br>▼ Expanding awareness through the body<br>▼ Mind-body connections<br>▼ Mimetic abilities<br>▼ Improved body functions | ■ Mimetic abilities: Role-play a job interview under various circumstances you might encounter.<br>■ Voluntary body movements: Experiment with ways to be aware of your body language, posture, and facial expressions to communicate during an interview.<br>■ Improved body functions: Practice various skills you need to perform a certain job. |
| **Naturalist Intelligence** | | ▼ Communion with nature<br>▼ Sensitivity to nature's flora<br>▼ Ability to care for, tame, and interact with living creatures<br>▼ Appreciating nature's impact<br>▼ Species classification | ■ Appreciating nature's impact: Analyze the impact a potential job's environment might have on you.<br>■ Species classification: Recognize various personality types within a workplace and list ways to work with those people.<br>■ Growing things: Recognize ways plants including flowers can affect work environments and mood. |

# Unit Stretching in High School
## Journey to Employment

| | Already Teach (MI capacities already part of the unit plan) | Multiple Intelligences Capacities Inventory | New Opportunities (additional MI capacities to be included in the plan) |
|---|---|---|---|
| **Verbal-Linguistic Intelligence** | | ▼ Understanding the order and meaning of words<br>▼ Explaining, teaching, and learning<br>▼ Linguistic humor<br>▼ Convincing someone to take a course of action<br>▼ Memory and recall<br>▼ Metalinguistic analysis | ■ Understanding the order and meaning of words: Learn appropriate vocabulary of the business world, including idioms.<br>■ Convincing someone to take a course of action: Practice convincing a potential employer that you're the one for the job.<br>■ Metalinguistic analysis: Study various nuances of business language or language that may be part of a job interview. |
| **Auditory-Vibrational Intelligence** (musical-rhythmic) | | ▼ Appreciation for the structure of music and rhythm<br>▼ Schemas or frames for hearing music and rhythm<br>▼ Sensitivity to sound<br>▼ Recognition, creation, and reproduction of melody, rhythm, and sound<br>▼ Recognizing characteristic qualities of tones and rhythm | ■ Recognizing characteristic qualities of tone and rhythm: Develop sensitivity to tonal qualities, pitch, timbre, and rhythm of one's own or another's speech.<br>■ Schemas or frames for hearing music and rhythm: Make music, rhythm, sound, and vibrational associations with the workplace.<br>■ Appreciation of the structure of music and rhythm: Use music and rhythm to shift your mood to look forward to filling out an application. |
| **Interpersonal Intelligence** | | ▼ Effective verbal and nonverbal communication<br>▼ Accurately reading others' moods, temperaments, motivations, and feelings<br>▼ Working cooperatively in a group<br>▼ Listening to and appreciating another's perspective<br>▼ Passing into the life of another<br>▼ Creating and maintaining synergy | ■ Effective verbal and nonverbal communication: Practice listening between the lines on a job interview and analyze your own intended communication.<br>■ Creating and maintaining synergy: Study and practice what's involved in creating or being a member of an effective team effort.<br>■ Accurately reading others' moods, temperaments, motivations, and feelings: Learn to pay attention to the nonobvious feedback on a job interview. |
| **Intrapersonal Intelligence** | | ▼ Concentration<br>▼ Mindfulness<br>▼ Metacognition<br>▼ Awareness and expression of various feelings<br>▼ Transpersonal sense of the self<br>▼ Higher-order thinking and reasoning | ■ Transpersonal sense of the self: Understand and communicate the unique contributions you can make to a job in the want ads.<br>■ Metacognition: Learn to track your own thinking processes and to shift from one mode of thinking to another.<br>■ Concentration of the mind: Practice staying absolutely focused on a task, not allowing yourself to be distracted. |

# Unit Stretching Work Sheet

**Unit Name** _____

## Objectives and Outcomes
What are the key concepts and skills you want to address?

## Room Arrangements
What various spaces for groups and individuals do you require?

## Resources
What materials, equipment, supplies, speakers, videos, and so on do you need?

## Assessment
What multimodal projects will you require of students to evaluate their learning?

# Unit Stretching Work Sheet

| | Already Teach (MI capacities already part of the unit plan) | Multiple Intelligences Capacities Inventory | New Opportunities (additional MI capacities to be included in the plan) |
|---|---|---|---|
| Visual-Spatial Intelligence | | ▼ Active imagination<br>▼ Forming mental images<br>▼ Finding own way in space<br>▼ Graphic representation<br>▼ Recognition of relationships between objects in space<br>▼ Image manipulation<br>▼ Accurate perception from various angles | |
| Logical-Mathematical Intelligence | | ▼ Abstract pattern recognition<br>▼ Inductive reasoning<br>▼ Deductive reasoning<br>▼ Discerning relationships and connections<br>▼ Performing complex calculations<br>▼ Scientific thinking | |

# Unit Stretching Work Sheet

| | Already Teach (MI capacities already part of the unit plan) | Multiple Intelligences Capacities Inventory | New Opportunities (additional MI capacities to be included in the plan) |
|---|---|---|---|
| **Bodily-Kinesthetic Intelligence** | | ▼ Voluntary body movements<br>▼ Preprogrammed body movements<br>▼ Expanding awareness through the body<br>▼ Mind-body connections<br>▼ Mimetic abilities<br>▼ Improved body functions | |
| **Naturalist Intelligence** | | ▼ Communion with nature<br>▼ Sensitivity to nature's flora<br>▼ Ability to care for, tame, and interact with living creatures<br>▼ Appreciating nature's impact<br>▼ Species classification | |

# Unit Stretching Work Sheet

| | Already Teach (MI capacities already part of the unit plan) | Multiple Intelligences Capacities Inventory | New Opportunities (additional MI capacities to be included in the plan) |
|---|---|---|---|
| Verbal-Linguistic Intelligence | | ▼ Understanding the order and meaning of words <br> ▼ Explaining, teaching, and learning <br> ▼ Linguistic humor <br> ▼ Convincing someone to take a course of action <br> ▼ Memory and recall <br> ▼ Metalinguistic analysis | |
| Auditory-Vibrational Intelligence (Musical-Rhythmic) | | ▼ Appreciation for the structure of music and rhythm <br> ▼ Schemas or frames for hearing music and rhythm <br> ▼ Sensitivity to sound <br> ▼ Recognition, creation, and reproduction of melody, rhythm, and sound <br> ▼ Recognizing characteristic qualities of tones and rhythm | |

# Unit Stretching Work Sheet

| | **Already Teach** (MI capacities already part of the unit plan) | **Multiple Intelligences Capacities Inventory** | **New Opportunities** (additional MI capacities to be included in the plan) |
|---|---|---|---|
| **Interpersonal Intelligence** | | ▼ Effective verbal and nonverbal communication<br><br>▼ Accurately reading others' moods, temperaments, motivations, and feelings<br><br>▼ Working cooperatively in a group<br><br>▼ Listening to and appreciating another's perspective<br><br>▼ Passing into the life of another<br><br>▼ Creating and maintaining synergy | |
| **Intrapersonal Intelligence** | | ▼ Concentration<br><br>▼ Mindfulness<br><br>▼ Metacognition<br><br>▼ Awareness and expression of various feelings<br><br>▼ Transpersonal sense of the self<br><br>▼ Higher-order thinking and reasoning | |

# Unit Stretching
# Reflection Log

### Other units I could apply this model to:

### Modifications I would make to this model:

### Things I particularly like about this model:

### The biggest challenges I anticipate in using this model:

# 5

# MI Stations or Learning Centers

*O*ne of the greatest rewards of my Multiple Intelligence teaching has been observing students work in their areas of strength through their independent projects. Many teachers face a dilemma when attempting to integrate Gardner's theory into their classrooms. They wonder whether to emphasize teaching through the seven [now eight!] intelligences on a daily basis or whether to nurture individual student strengths. I choose to do both . . .

Ultimately, I believe that students working in an MI environment develop new strengths and come to better understand and appreciate themselves as individuals. Because of the skills the students develop, they have multiple abilities to pursue their interests long after they leave my classroom. And that has always been my goal as an educator: to inspire a love of learning in each child I teach.

—Bruce Campbell
*The Multiple Intelligences Handbook* (137, 167)

I call this model the "MI Stations" or the "MI Learning Centers model." Throughout this chapter, I will simply refer to it as the "MI Stations model." The use of stations and learning centers to integrate MI into the curriculum has been successful in a number of school districts across the country. It is based on the work of Bruce Campbell, an elementary teacher in the Marysville School District in Washington State.

## Purpose of the MI Stations Model

The main intent of the MI Stations model is to provide students with opportunities to process information in a unit in a wide variety of unique and creative ways.

## Goals of the MI Stations Model

- To provide students with a safe environment in which to practice using the various capacities of the intelligences
- To provide students with opportunities to explore and understand the various concepts of a unit in a variety of ways by using all the intelligences
- To move students' learning beyond the mere memorization and consequent recitation of facts, figures, and so on into realms of higher-order thinking and processing
- To help students discover, tap, enjoy, and further develop their own and one another's creativity!

## The Development of the MI Stations Model

Bruce Campbell developed one version of this model in Washington State. He set up one center for each intelligence and named it for a person who is famous for that intelligence. Students work on a concept at all the centers during the morning, then work on individual projects of their choosing in the afternoon.

Following is his description of what a classroom based on the "stations model" might look like:

> Three eight- and nine-year-old boys recently gave an oral report about California to their classmates. The students sang and danced an original song about the state, played a short video they produced, displayed maps drawn to scale, and spiritedly presented a series of facts. Are these students academically advanced or exceptionally

creative? No, such multimodal learning is commonplace in a third-fourth-fifth grade multiaged classroom at Cascade Elementary School in Marysville, Washington.

Inspired by Howard Gardner's theory of multiple intelligences, this classroom features learning centers, each devoted to one of the intelligences identified by Gardner. The students spend approximately two-thirds of their day rotating through the various stations. The morning begins with a brief lecture and discussion of the classroom's current theme. Students then divide into groups of approximately four children each to begin center work. The class spends 20 to 30 minutes at each center, learning about the day's topic through all the intelligences. (Campbell 1993, 1)

In this same article Bruce also describes what takes place at the various centers, all of which have been named after famous people whose lives reflect the intelligences to help children understand further the various intelligences:

In a recent unit on outer space, the class studied comets for a day. In the Martha Graham Center [bodily-kinesthetic intelligence], students made model comets with sticks, marshmallows, and ribbons, and choreographed dances illustrating a comet's orbit around the Sun. Using school textbooks in the William Shakespeare Center [verbal-linguistic intelligence], students read about comets, and in the Albert Einstein Center [logical-mathematical intelligence], solved story problems concerning the lengths of a comet's tail. In the Mother Teresa Center [interpersonal intelligence], each group collaboratively created a database file of comet facts in the classroom's computer. In the Emily Dickinson Center, students individually authored poems on pieces of paper cut to resemble comets. Colorful comets were designed with glue and glitter in graph paper and comet parts were labeled and drawn in proportion at the Pablo Picasso Center. In the Ray Charles Center, each group created a song incorporating several comet facts. At the end of the day, comet poems were bound in a class book, songs were performed by each group, art work was displayed on a bulletin board, and progress in the other centers shared. (3)

Basically, you set up the stations or learning centers with intelligence-appropriate learning tasks in each. Provide students with whatever introductory material is necessary to get them started. Then place them in teams to explore and discover the remainder of the unit (and the learning!) in a very hands-on fashion in each station, interacting with the material by performing the learning tasks. To end the unit, the class gathers and the various teams share their new learnings about the topic and the products they created in the centers. I don't mean to imply that every concept involved in a unit will be studied via all eight centers. However, I do suggest that during the unit, students visit all of the centers at some point.

## Things about This Model That Excite and Interest Me

■ *It is easily adaptable to any topic.* Although at first glance it may seem more appropriate for elementary students, with a couple of adjustments it can work very well at the middle school and high school levels. See pages 132–43 and my discussion of them for examples of these adaptations. Of all of the curriculum integration models presented in this book, the MI Stations model is easiest to adapt to any grade level and to any curricular content. Once you have articulated your objectives and outcomes for the unit, you then simply craft the stations around achieving those objectives and outcomes, selecting those capacities that will suit those objectives.

Initially, planning the stations may seem like a nightmare, but once they are in place, you can use them over and over again throughout the year. The most difficult part of using this model is acquiring the materials needed in each station so that the media of the intelligence is readily available to the students.

■ *It is a very student-centered approach to learning.* The dynamics of this model are very student centered, even when and if the teacher basically plans the various learning tasks for the centers. Students must still take the initial ideas and build on them, expand on them, and use them to create knowledge for themselves. This model is very much in line with current constructivist approaches to the curriculum as well as with problem-based learning. In both approaches, students must interact with, use, and find meaning in the material they are studying. They are not simply passive recipients of whatever the teacher doles out.

In several schools, I have encountered students who are actively involved in setting up the centers and even in planning the respective learning tasks, which offers students at least two benefits. They feel ownership right up front, which generally generates their excitement and anticipation about the unit. And getting students involved in planning the individual station's learning tasks is an excellent way to educate students about the intelligences and what is involved in using each of them to enhance and deepen their learning.

■ *It offers a great way to use cooperative groups.* The MI Stations model demonstrates one of the most effective ways I know to use cooperative groups in the classroom. I do not feel that you must use a cooperative group approach, but I believe that the excitement will be greater and students' learning will be greatly amplified because they may learn as much from one another and from the team's interaction with the material as they do from the material itself.

It is important to mention that, if you choose to use cooperative groups to explore the stations, it is very important to spend some time teaching students ways to be effective in groups, such as assigning roles, bonding, teaching social skills, ensuring individual accountability, and so on. I also suggest you review all your training in cooperative learning and the research that has documented ways to set up the teams for success.

■ *The learning is open ended.* While you have certain learning goals for the unit, given that students are working directly with the material, the learning can go far beyond what you initially anticipate. As students work in each of the stations, they will raise many questions about the topic, some of which you could in no way have anticipated. Human learning is not a neat, linear affair. It is messy. Sometimes chaotic. Frequently unpredictable. And real learning is always transformational. Our own concepts of ourselves and of our world change, often dramatically. As students enter the various stations, they enter this whirlwind of learning. Your role is to facilitate the process, to act as coach. But the learning occurs not as you impart wisdom, but as students question, struggle, play, explore, and interact with the material via the various center activities.

## The Basic Process

Following are steps for using the MI Stations work sheet (see pages 144 through 145). Students are divided into teams that travel around to the various stations or learning centers.

**Step 1**  Set up one learning center, exploration center, or laboratory for each intelligence. Include the actual media of the intelligence. In many cases, the mere presence of these media can evoke the intelligence! The examples on pages 122 through 123 suggest some of the items you might include in the various stations; however, remember that these are only beginning suggestions and not an exhaustive list.

**Step 2**  Determine the curriculum concepts you want students to understand by the time they are through with the unit; determine also the skills you want them to master in and through the unit. Clearly outline the knowledge base.

**Step 3**  On the MI Capacities Wheels (pages 19 and 20), target the various capacities for each intelligence you think will help students explore the various concepts most effectively. Then, from those capacities, choose one for each station that will be the focus of the learning tasks. Match concepts and skills with the various stations.

**Step 4**  Using the unique media of the intelligence and, more specifically, the targeted capacity (see chart on pages 122 and 123), plan a series of required learning tasks to help students understand the key concepts.

You may also offer a variety of learning tasks and ask students to choose the ones they want to complete. If students are comfortable with and knowledgeable about the intelligences, you may want them to come up with their own ideas that focus on the capacities.

**Step 5**  Decide how much time students will need in each station to perform the activities you have planned. As much as possible, give equal time to complete the activities in the stations. Depending on the unit, the time frame could be anywhere from one period to several days in each station or center.

**Step 6**  Assign center exploration teams. Again, I suggest a team approach because not only is it easier for you to stay on top of what is going on, but also research tells us that with cooperative learning, students' understanding and mastery of concepts and skills are likely to be enhanced.

**Step 7**  Monitor! Monitor!! Monitor!!! Once the teams are involved in the stations, your main job is to monitor the students. Make sure students don't get stuck. Ensure that their understanding is accurate (that is, they working with correct information). Watch the group dynamics to make sure all students do their parts, support one another, and so on. Note questions they are generating and point them in directions to explore further.

**Step 8**  At the end of the unit, when all teams have visited all the stations, allow time not only for sharing the products produced in the various centers, but also for discussion of what they have learned and their new questions.

## Project Media and Ideas

### Verbal-Linguistic

The station should include paper, pencils, pens, dictionaries, thesaurus, tape recorder, typewriter or word processor, poetry books, joke books, magazines, and other written materials.

**PROJECT IDEAS** ...............

- ★ Writing essays or reports
- ★ Writing poetry and limericks
- ★ Defining key vocabulary words
- ★ Formal speaking (persuasive or explanatory)
- ★ Debating

### Visual-Spatial

The station should include paints, colored markers, clay, videos, colored construction paper, building blocks, Legos™, maps, posters, books and magazines with a lot of pictures, scissors, and paste.

**PROJECT IDEAS** ...............

- ★ Creating graphic illustrations (pictures and murals)
- ★ Making sculptures (clay and dirt)
- ★ Creating montages and collages
- ★ Making flowcharts
- ★ Designing posters and brochures

### Logical-Mathematical

The station should include calculators, computers, rulers, and books containing graphic organizers.

**PROJECT IDEAS** ...............

- ★ Creating annotated outlines
- ★ Reporting statistics
- ★ Demonstrating thinking patterns such as comparison/contrast
- ★ Explaining the steps involved in a process

### Bodily-Kinesthetic

The station should include costumes, makeup, sports equipment, and material for building or inventing something.

**PROJECT IDEAS** ...............

- ★ Creating a drama, role-play, or mime
- ★ Dancing (both traditional and creative or original)
- ★ Creating human tableaux
- ★ Creating physical routines (body language, gestures, exercise)
- ★ Building something

# Musical-Rhythmic

The station should include musical instruments, percussion instruments, audiocassette players, a variety of music and sound tapes, and various kinds of noisemakers.

## PROJECT IDEAS . . . . . . . . . . . . . . . .

★ Creating a musical TV ad or jingle
★ Creating a sound accompaniment on tape
★ Writing songs (original or known tunes)
★ Exploring rhythmic and beat factors (cultures, seasons, body processes)

# Intrapersonal

This station should include solitary, quiet space to walk; blank paper for journal entries, sets of journal writing "starters" (see *Seven Pathways of Learning*), a list of self-reflective questions to consider

## PROJECT IDEAS . . . . . . . . . . . . . . .

★ Writing autobiographies
★ Writing or drawing in personal, reflective journals
★ Doing thinking logs
★ Keeping self-understanding diaries

# Interpersonal

This station should include lists of things to do with a partner, group projects, things to talk about, and suggestions for working together.

## PROJECT IDEAS . . . . . . . . . . . . . . .

★ Doing think-pair-share (see *Pathways of Learning*)
★ Putting together a jigsaw project with a team
★ Doing each one teach one (see *Pathways of Learning*)
★ Competing on teams
★ Taking questionnaires and surveys

# Naturalist

This station should include as many objects from the natural world as possible: rocks, leaves, bark, animal fur, plants; even better, students go outside and gather their own objects.

## PROJECT IDEAS . . . . . . . . . . . . . . .

★ Creating a diorama using all natural elements
★ Recording environmental sounds on an audiocassette
★ Creating a photographic display
★ Making collages, dyes, paper, and so on, from natural elements
★ Videotaping scenes, animals, weather conditions, and so on

## Evaluations of the Model

Following are some of my own thoughts about the pluses and minuses of the MI Stations model. I hope you and your colleagues will engage in a similar evaluation of this model in your department, school, or district to find the approach that is best suited to your situation.

### + + +  PLUSES  + + +

▶ **This approach is already used in much early elementary education.** By its very nature, early childhood education and early childhood teachers know that you must incorporate a wide range of learning experiences, activities, and opportunities into a typical school day if you are to hold children's attention. Guess what? This concept applies to more than early childhood! I have discovered, through many years of conducting professional development workshops for adults, that adult learners need variety, as well. Given our bioneurological makeup, every human, regardless of age, needs a wide range of experiences to learn!

▶ **It is easy to adapt to any unit.** As I mentioned earlier, the MI Stations model is one of the most adaptable models for anything you are trying to teach. The task is basically to brainstorm learning activities for *each* station that will access the targeted capacity of the individual intelligences. There are three steps in preparing for this model: know the capacities and what is involved in tapping them (see chapter 2 of this book as well as *Eight Ways of Knowing* by David Lazear); brainstorm a healthy list of learning strategies, tools, techniques, activities, games, processes, and so on, for each intelligence; and focus these strategies, tools, activities, on the targeted capacities.

▶ **The materials (or what I have called the "media") of the intelligences are readily available.** The materials, equipment, and resources for implementing this approach are easy to come by. They are readily available at very low prices at local department stores. The key is to ensure that you get the various media in the centers before you begin the unit.

## – – – **MINUSES** – – –

▶ **It takes time and some expense to plan and set up.** It is time consuming at first to plan and set up the stations or learning centers. It will also likely take some outlay of money, although not a large amount. But bear in mind that, once the centers are set up, you can then use them many times during the year with little or no further planning.

▶ **It requires a bit of space.** The small classroom or a classroom that has other physical constraints, such as bolted-down desks or stationary tables, can challenge your implementation of this model. Generally, the elementary classroom space is more flexible and adaptable than middle and high school classrooms. However, teachers in some middle schools and high schools have rearranged their rooms to make them more conducive to setting up stations or have created special places or rooms in the school that they schedule as stations.

▶ **In the secondary years, periods generally are not long enough unless block scheduled.** The forty-five-minute period creates some definite challenges to the use of the MI Stations model. It is next to impossible to have students get around to all the stations within the period. However, it would be possible to do a station a day or to allow students to choose the station in which they want to work each day, as long as you require that they visit all the stations during the course of the unit. I address some of the difficulties and adaptations for middle school and high school in my commentaries on the examples.

▶ **Possibility of misunderstanding that the model is meant to teach everything using all eight intelligences.** I personally believe that, *in principle,* everything can be taught using all the intelligences, although that is not what I advocate here, nor is it what my inclusion of this model is meant to suggest. Rather, at the heart of this model is the suggestion that students need a wide range of learning experiences to deeply understand anything we want them to learn.

# Elementary

### General Science: Mammals

This example illustrates how to use the MI Stations model to teach an elementary general science unit on mammals. The unit deals with all aspects of understanding mammals and their world, including where they live, ways they care for their young, ways they live together, and so on.

## Academic Objectives and Outcomes

● To understand what makes a mammal a mammal (as opposed to a reptile, for example), and to learn the names of various mammals and their distinguishing characteristics

● To understand key facts about various families of mammals, including habitat, food, mating patterns, skeletal structure, body coverings, hunting habits, reproductive systems, and care for the young

● To be able to classify various species into groups of mammals (for example, "the cat family" or "the wolf family"), and to explain the reasons the classification is accurate

● To learn how to care for, train, and relate to various kinds of mammals in appropriate ways

● To explore the past, present, and future roles of mammals in society and in students' individual and family lives

The example assumes a month-long unit, although, obviously, students won't be doing the centers all day, every day. Notice that I have targeted one capacity in each station, then provided a variety of activities that are more or less in line with helping students use the specific capacity and strengthen that aspect of the given intelligence. In other words, they exercise one capacity for each intelligence, so to speak, in the learning of the material involved in the unit.

The learning tasks in each of the stations or centers were designed so they could be completed in about one hour. I assume that students would not perform all tasks in each station; however, if you have the time, I believe giving students time to do each of the learning tasks will enhance and further develop the overall concepts of the unit. Teams could also divide the various tasks among the team members, or you could require they perform two activities of their own choice. Please study the example (page 131) before beginning.

## Commentary on the Elementary MI Stations Model Example

General science in the elementary years (especially the early years!) is a true delight, for children's natural curiosity about the world and the desire to explore it are still very much alive. Likewise, generally all of the intelligences are also still alive. So using MI to further this curiosity and exploratory drive is almost like a hand-in-glove fit. The MI Stations model also fits well with the very nature of elementary education: classrooms tend to be more or less self-contained, generally you are working with the same group of students throughout the day, and, especially in recent years, elementary teachers are being given more flexibility in how their classrooms will be run as long as students master the required material.

Following are some of my reflections, thoughts, insights, and other "metacognitive postscripts and ramblings" on the example.

- The learning process involved in using this model is based in exploration, discovery, curiosity, and problem solving. It is much less focused on "right answers" and much more on the process of student inquiry. I'm not suggesting that students should not be corrected when and if their explorations lead them to inaccurate conclusions or information; however, I must say that some of the greatest learning in my own life has come from having to correct errors or figure out what was wrong with a solution. The very nature of a learning center invites students to follow various pathways of inquiry based on the material being studied. In some ways, the "stuff" of the curriculum is but a springboard to a deeper understanding of oneself and one's world. The outcome or destination of learning center explorations is less certain than other methods, but also much more exciting and engaging.

- Something I mentioned in the steps of the process above bears repeating here. Your role in managing this process is that of facilitator of the stations and coach when, for example, questions are evoked, confusions arise, fuzzy thinking or conclusions are drawn, and so on. Facilitating this process is obviously quite different from doing so in more traditional direct instruction. As the teams visit the various stations, your job is to monitor their progress and, even more important, the process of learning and understanding that is occurring; that is, you must continually ask yourself, "Are my objectives and outcomes being achieved?"

- As you set up the stations and prepare to use them in a unit, you must ask yourself several questions to make some decisions:

  ➤ Are students going to explore in teams, as individuals, as partners, or a combination of these?

  ➤ How much choice and how many options will I offer at each station?

  ➤ What *performance rubrics* related to the learning tasks should I develop?

  ➤ What *content rubrics* will give me feedback to ensure students are in fact learning and understanding the required material?

  ➤ How much time will students need to spend in each station to complete the activities and thoroughly master the concepts?

  ➤ How will you decide these things? Return to your articulation of the objectives and outcomes for the unit, which will more or less dictate the directions you take.

- The most difficult part of planning the various learning tasks is to make sure that they match the curriculum and the targeted MI capacities. Chapter 2 will help you create capacity-targeted learning tasks. My book *Eight Ways of Knowing* provides further explanation of the capacities as well as exercises that can help you understand what is involved in working with each capacity.

- In the steps for using this process I suggest that you not only target the appropriate capacities but also that you match the content with the appropriate learning center. While I believe this approach will give you something like a checklist to ensure that you deal with all concepts in a unit, there may be times when this approach is not appropriate. Some concepts may need to be the focus of several, if not all, of the stations. A third option, the one I used in the example, is more of a "scatter gun" approach: the concepts are spread across the stations in such a way that students deal with the same concept in two to three different stations.

# MI Learning Stations and Centers
## Elementary Unit
## Mammals

## Visual-Spatial Station
**Targeted capacity: Graphic representation**

- Find pictures of mammals in magazines and make a montage.
- Make a diorama of various mammal habitats.
- Paint or draw mammals and their food.
- Sculpt the skeletons of various mammals.

## Intrapersonal Station
**Targeted capacity: Awareness of and expression of various feelings**

- Imagine you are a mammal and you have human emotions; what angers you, makes you happy, and so on?
- Think about feelings you have for various living creatures.
- Study ways you can tell what an animal might be feeling.

## Interpersonal Station
**Targeted capacity: Effective verbal and nonverbal communication**

- Listen to a partner's information or story about mammals, then repeat it to another.
- Pretend you are a nonhuman mammal communicating with a human; what would you do to get your point across?
- Individually research a mammal, then tell a group about your findings.

## Bodily-Kinesthetic Station
**Targeted capacity: Control of voluntary body movements**

- Practice moving the way various mammals move (walking, running, swimming) in the manners they move.
- Imagine you are a mammal caring for your young; act out what is involved.
- Create a game based on mammal movements that involves making the movements and adding on to the movements of others.

## Auditory-Vibrational (Musical-Rhythmic) Station
**Targeted capacity: Sensitivity to sounds**

- Play name that mammal based on the sounds they make.
- Learn the sounds various mammals make to express their wants, states of being, and so on.
- Create an audiotape that includes the sounds of mammals in their environment.

## Logical-Mathematical Station
**Targeted capacity: Discerning relationships and connections**

- Create webs of mammals' food chains and life cycles.
- Make a matrix that shows animals' adaptations and probable causes.
- Use Venn diagrams to compare mammals.
- Predict causes and effects of various mammal behaviors.

## Naturalist Station
**Targeted capacity: Classifying species**

- Go for a nature walk and look for certain groupings of mammals.
- Through firsthand encounters, understand reasons certain animal classifications apply.
- Create a mammal classification game that includes habitats, foods, mating, and so on.

## Verbal-Linguistic Station
**Targeted capacity: Memory and recall**

- Learn vocabulary words related to the world and life of mammals.
- Make up and work mammal-related crosswords or other word games.
- Brainstorm a list of everything you know and want to know about various mammals.
- Match various mammals with the appropriate facts and information about them.

# Middle School

## History Unit: The American Revolution

This example illustrates how to use the MI Stations model to teach a unit on America's struggle for independence at the middle school level. Generally, this topic is not one about which a typical middle school student is dying to find out! In fact, they are not interested in most parts of the required curriculum in the middle school years. The example that follows is an attempt to demonstrate a way to use MI to juice up this unit and create more interest and excitement about learning the material.

## Academic Objectives and Outcomes

- To understand the key causes of the American Revolution, including historical trends and events that coalesced in each cause, and how and why each caused the Revolution

- To understand the key figures behind the American Revolution, including factors that shaped people's temperament and thinking, their main ideas and thoughts, key dates and other relevant biographical data, and factors that led them to take action in the struggle for independence

- To grasp key dates and events, and understand why these are important and how they affected the larger struggle for independence

- To see connections between American Revolutionary times and life in America today, including contemporary struggles over the Bill of Rights

- To reflect on connections between one's own personal journey and America's journey to independence, for example, how one's everyday life would be different had the Revolution not occurred

The example assumes the unit will span several weeks. The unit would obviously work best in a block or intensive schedule; however, in my commentary on the example, I discuss ways to effectively conduct this approach in a limited amount of time, forty-five minutes or less. Again, I have zeroed in on one capacity in each station, providing a variety of intelligence-specific learning experiences that will help students use the various capacities while they are processing the curricular material. In the process of their learning, they will enhance, strengthen, and develop certain dimensions or aspects of the intelligence by exercising its capacities (very much like what you might do to improve your serve in tennis).

Following the example (page 131) is a discussion of the unit as I've presented it, including suggestions for adapting the process, given the unique challenges of teaching middle school students, and some options of other ways to use the model. Please study the example before beginning.

### Commentary on the Middle School MI Stations Model Example

Recently in a workshop I met a history teacher who told me he taught history backward. When I asked him to explain, he told me that he starts with today, then peels off the layers of history one at a time. He said that his students never lose sight of how the past has shaped the present. When you approach teaching history using multiple intelligences, you offer many, many ways that will help students understand the meaning of the past for their lives today.

Following are some of my reflections, thoughts, insights, and other "metacognitive postscripts and ramblings" on the example I have presented.

■ As students approach secondary education, it becomes more and more important to teach them about their many ways of knowing, acquiring knowledge, processing information, understanding, and learning. The unique life changes that happen to middle school students make them ripe for learning about their intelligences. In and through their participation in the stations, their knowledge about themselves and their ways of knowing definitely grow.

In some ways teaching students about MI represents the metacognitive aspect of the theory. While doing so does not really add to the content, it is a reflective and processing dimension through which we ask students to be aware of the learning process. The multiple intelligences become a parallel curriculum. (See *Pathways of Learning* for more on this topic.)

■ If you are not teaching in a block or other schedule in which you have students for long periods of time, you can still use the MI Stations model. A middle school teacher in Michigan was teaching forty-two-minute periods, and she did not even have her own classroom. She was in a different room every period. But she really loved the MI Stations model and told me, "I'm going to figure out a way to adapt it to this impossible situation!" She loaded eight separate suitcases with all the media of the intelligences. She related her experience of working with this model as follows: "I would fly into my office between periods and grab the appropriate suitcase. When I got to class, I would throw open the suitcase and pull out the appropriate stuff, much like the medicine man who used to come to town in the old West; it was show time!" She told me, "My students live in holy terror of what I might pull out of the suitcase each day!"

In a nutshell, this teacher took the stations to the students rather than the students going to the stations. Every three days or so, she would bring a suitcase with the materials of a different station to her classroom.

■ Other schools have designated rooms or special areas for the various stations; for example, the art room becomes the visual-spatial room or the music room, the auditory-vibrational room, and so on. Teachers schedule a "station room" to teach students a learning task connected with a unit. All students travel to a particular station room and work at the same station for two to three days. You can still divide them into exploration teams to work on various targeted capacities.

■ In my commentary on the elementary example, I mention the power of having students involved not only in setting up the stations, but also in planning the various learning tasks. Such an approach is very appropriate for middle school students as well. Students at this stage of development need independence. They need to have some say over what happens to them in their lives. They seek fun, freedom, a sense of belonging, and a sense of power, and they have a desire to fit in with and be accepted by their peers (see William Glasser's work on control theory for more information). The MI Stations model is almost tailor-made to address these needs.

■ I am not making suggestions that you change the content, or that you *should* be teaching students about the American Revolution. My goal is to illustrate the use of the MI Stations model by using content that would be appropriate and often is part of middle school curriculum.

## MI Learning Stations and Centers
## Middle School Unit
## The American Revolution

### Visual-Spatial Station

**Targeted capacity: Recognizing relationships between objects in space**

- Create a map that shows strategies and progression of the war.
- Design displays that show the location of and relationships among key events.
- Design a flowchart that shows the increasing divergent view of the American Colonists and the British.

### Intrapersonal Station

**Targeted capacity: Transpersonal sense of self**

- Experience various perspectives of the struggle (British, colonists, children, and so on)
- Write a comparative journal entry on "My Revolution and the American Revolution."
- Imagine ways your life would be different if the American Revolution had not occurred.

### Interpersonal Station

**Targeted capacity: Working cooperatively in a group**

- In teams, create presentations that show the causes of the American Revolution.
- In expert groups, study the stages of the Revolution and present your findings to the class.
- Jigsaw key figures in the Revolution and document their roles in the struggle (that is, divide the research among group members).

### Bodily-Kinesthetic Station

**Targeted capacity: Mimetic abilities**

- Dramatize some key battles or events in the struggle for independence.
- Act out a typical life in colonial America, then the same life after the Revolution.
- Role-play a revolutionary figure dealing with a current issue or problem.

### Auditory-Vibrational (Musical-Rhythmic) Station

**Targeted capacity: Recognition, creation, and production of melody, rhythm, and sound**

- Learn songs of the Revolution, then write some of your own.
- Tell the story of America's struggle for independence in sound, music, and rhythm.
- Create a radio show that reports on the Revolution.

### Logical-Mathematical Station

**Targeted capacity: Inductive and deductive reasoning**

- Analyze the thought patterns of the key figures behind the American Revolution.
- Analyze the thought patterns of key players on the British side.
- Analyze thought patterns of today's leaders as if they were leading during the Revolution.

### Naturalist Station

**Targeted capacity: Communion with nature**

- Study and understand ways the environment influenced the American Revolution.
- Understand and demonstrate ways the patriots used the natural world.
- Analyze nature looking for change processes that remind you of the struggle during the American Revolution.

### Verbal-Linguistic Station

**Targeted capacity: Understanding the order and meaning of words**

- Analyze the meanings of words and phrases in revolutionary essays and documents.
- Deliver revolutionary speeches in ways that embody their meaning and stir the soul.
- Rewrite the Declaration of Independence in language your classmates would understand and relate to.

# Multiple Intelligence Stations

# *High School*

## Civics: Forms of Government

This example illustrates a way to use the MI Stations model to teach a high school civics unit on various forms of government in our contemporary world. The example illustrates a way to use MI to give students an in-depth, working understanding of key structures and dynamics present in any government, and, in so doing, increase their understanding of and appreciation for the form of government in their own nation.

## Academic Objectives and Outcomes

● To understand the basic definitions of various forms of government

● To explain the various forms of government using one's own language

● To understand the foundation, dynamics, and structures present in any form of government

● To identify the key characteristics of various forms of government and understand similarities and differences in ways the various branches function within them (for example, legislative, judiciary, and executive branches)

● To know where the various forms of government exist and to recognize key figures in the news who represent these governments

● To discuss key social problems in various nations and how their respective governments are handling them

● To compare and contrast the form of government in one's own nation with forms of government in other parts of the world, including pros and cons of one's own form of government based on its dealing with current national challenges, issues, and social problems

The example assumes the unit will take about one month. As with the middle school example, this one would obviously work best in a block or intensive schedule; however, in my commentary, I discuss ways you can implement the example in a typical forty- to fifty-minute period. I assign certain concepts to the stations or learning centers that are in synch with the concepts, then I target one capacity per station, again selecting capacities that seem to fit the concepts. Once these items are in place, namely the concepts and the MI capacities, I create a variety of intelligence-specific, hands-on experiences that will not only help students learn about various forms of government, but will also require their use of all eight intelligences during the course of the unit.

Following the example (page 143) is a discussion including suggestions for adapting the process, given the unique challenges of working with the complex material that is generally part of a high school curriculum, as well as the challenges of teaching today's high school students, or maybe more appropriately, today's young adults. Please study the example before beginning.

## Commentary on the High School MI Stations Model Example

Learning about the world's governments can be a very dry topic for any person, let alone high school students whose minds and attention are often focused anywhere but on the curriculum, no matter what the subject is. One big plus of using a multiple intelligence approach is that it comes at learning through many more doorways than what some have called "the sit and git" approach. By its very nature, the MI Stations model requires students to interact with the material. They simply do not have the option of being passive recipients, for the material will not be presented in that way. To "git it," they must actively seek it and make meaning out of it for themselves.

Following are some of my reflections, thoughts, insights, and other "metacognitive postscripts and ramblings" on the example.

- Whether or not you would, in fact, take a month on the concepts in the example is not my point. Nor am I making a content recommendation. The purpose of the example is to illustrate a way to use the MI Stations model with content that would be appropriate for and often is part of a high school civics curriculum. Some high school civics teachers I have met in workshops deal with such a unit as a thematic unit that spans an entire term, with the various civics concepts to be learned woven in and out of the learning process.

- The degree of your success in using the MI Stations with high school students will be directly proportional to their understanding of their own intelligence strengths. While you may need to make a slight addition of this material to the curriculum initially, the benefits students and you will reap from taking time to learn about the intelligences will definitely pay off. Students will see that MI can make school a more interesting and joyful experience. They will discover new ways to succeed at their studies. They will find a new esteem for their intellectual capacities, knowing that we are all stronger in some areas than others. And they will begin to learn that any weak or underdeveloped intelligence can indeed be enhanced and strengthened.

First, teach students that we all have at least eight ways of knowing, eight ways we acquire knowledge, process knowledge, learn, and understand. Second, not only tell them about the intelligences, but also help them discover the intelligences in themselves. Third, demonstrate that each intelligence is valid in its own right *and* that we value the use of the various intelligences in the classroom. Finally, give them some experience in using various intelligences to learn through the learning centers.

■ Using the MI Stations model in a block or intensive schedule is no problem. In an eighty- to ninety-minute period, students would obviously have plenty of time to delve deeply into the tasks at a station. In fact, depending on your objectives and outcomes, they could even work on learning tasks in several stations during one period. The biggest challenge in working with the MI Stations in the block or intensive schedule is to monitor students' work to ensure that they are on task, that they are doing quality work, and that they are dealing with all of the concepts you have slotted into the various stations.

■ Using the MI Stations in the traditional forty- to fifty-minute period presents another set of challenges, not the least of which is how much can be accomplished in such a limited amount of time, especially when working with a hands-on, experiential teaching/learning process. The key is in the planning. You will likely only be able to deal with one station at a time and its learning tasks during the period, and even then, this work will more than likely have to span several days for students to complete the learning tasks of the station. You must ensure that all the materials required are available and that students are clear on what the learning tasks are. When the period is over, students must have a moment to state what their next step will be when they return to the work.

I am not suggesting that it is impossible to have several stations going on simultaneously in the traditional forty- to fifty-minute period. Some teachers have divided students into three or four groups, with each group working on the learning tasks in one station at a time. Such an approach makes it a bit more difficult for you to monitor their work and learning, but it is workable, especially as students become increasingly comfortable with the various intelligences and with an inquiry, exploration approach to learning.

■ I could write an entire book on how to assess the learning that occurs in the MI Stations model. In fact, I have written two books on multiple intelligences and assessment. Allow me to attempt to capsulize the main points here.

➤ *The assessment must match the instruction.* In the case of MI Stations, students must be given opportunities to demonstrate what they have learned in any way they can (what I call multimodal assessment). To assess their real *understanding* of the material, require them to show what they know, that is, to represent their understanding in at least three different ways.

➤ *Once you know they understand the required material, ask them to transfer that understanding to formal tests or other situations.* Unfortunately, we do not have formal tests that allow students to perform their understanding. Or maybe to state it more accurately, most of our formal tests allow only two ways of performing, namely, verbal-linguistic and logical-mathematical. It is therefore part of our task to help students *transfer their understanding* to the mostly verbal-linguistic and logical-mathematical tests by which their learning will ultimately be judged.

➤ *You need two sets of scoring rubrics.* One set of rubrics is for the content; have they adequately proven their mastery of the required concepts, facts, figures, and so on? The second set of rubrics is to evaluate the intelligences and students' performance of the learning tasks in the station. The intelligence rubric should encourage students to perform at high levels regardless of the intelligence being used.

➤ *The assessment process should genuinely benefit students.* Assessment should not be something we do *to* students. It should be something we do *with* them. In fact, a really good assessment, one that is student and intelligence focused, is probably one of the best instructional strategies we have at our disposal. We can actually enhance and deepen students' learning in and through a great assessment.

For more information on what I have summarized here please see *Multiple Intelligence Approaches to Assessment* and *The Rubrics Way* (Lazear 1998c and 1998d, respectively).

## MI Learning Stations and Centers

### High School Unit
### Forms of Government

---

## Visual-Spatial Station

**Targeted capacity: Forming mental images**

- Picture various world leaders speaking to the public they govern; share what you see.
- Imagine your family living under a form of government different from the one you live under now; tell others what it's like.
- Visualize people under various governments dealing with a given social issue; explain to others what you see.

---

## Intrapersonal Station

**Targeted capacity: Higher-order thinking and reasoning**

- List values you think are key to various forms of government.
- Reflect on your positive and negative feelings about various governments.
- Consider ways various governments would solve current social problems in your nation. How would you feel about these solutions?

---

## Interpersonal Station

**Targeted capacity: Passing into the perspective of another**

- Understand why various nations have various perspectives on the same issues.
- Imagine you are a citizen in a nation different from the one in which you currently live. What would be your view of your nation?
- Reflect on how your life would be different under another form of government.

---

## Bodily-Kinesthetic Station

**Targeted capacity: Mind-body connections**

- Create movements, gestures, facial expressions, and so on that reflect various governments.
- Note bodily reactions to images, sounds, words, and so on from various governments.
- Create human tableaux or living sculptures to illustrate the key values of various governments.

---

## Auditory-Vibrational (Musical-Rhythmic) Station

**Targeted capacity: Characteristic qualities of tones and rhythm**

- Associate various sounds, rhythms, and so on with various forms of government.
- Analyze national anthems and how they reflect respective governments.
- Listen to, discuss, and analyze the pitch, timbre, tone, volume, and inflection of various leaders addressing their people as opposed to the actual words they use.

---

## Logical-Mathematical Station

**Targeted capacity: Scientific reasoning**

- Experiment with solving a problem as various governments might try to solve it.
- Uncover the assumptions behind various governments' positions on current issues.
- Plan negotiations with various governments as if you were their leaders.

---

## Naturalist Station

**Targeted capacity: Appreciating nature's impact**

- Study ways various environments have influenced the development of various governments.
- Study and evaluate various governments' environmental protection programs.
- Study ways various governments utilize or exploit the natural world.

---

## Verbal-Linguistic Station

**Targeted capacity: Convincing others to take a specific course of action**

- Conduct debates on the pros and cons of various forms of government.
- Write essays on the merits of a government that is quite different from your own.
- Write position papers on human rights from the perspectives of various governments.

## MI
## Learning Stations and Centers
Planning Work Sheet

**Visual-Spatial Station**
Targeted capacity:

**Intrapersonal Station**
Targeted capacity:

**Interpersonal Station**
Targeted capacity:

**Bodily-Kinesthetic Station**
Targeted capacity:

**Auditory-Vibrational (Musical-Rhythmic) Station**
Targeted capacity:

**Logical-Mathematical Station**
Targeted capacity:

**Naturalist Station**
Targeted capacity:

**Verbal-Linguistic Station**
Targeted capacity:

# MI Stations or Learning Centers
# Reflection Log

### Other units I could apply this model to:

### Modifications I would make to this model:

### Things I particularly like about this model:

### The biggest challenges I anticipate in using this model:

# 6
# Schoolwide Focus

*MI in the Spotlight*

*I* have been astonished how frequently a teacher of one age group
has no idea of what the students did the previous year and no
idea what they will be doing the following year; it is as if each year
were sacrosanct and one were supposed to begin each fall "from
scratch" . . . What was done in math or English last year is not
considered to be related to the task for the coming year; and tips
about writing picked up, say, in history class, are rarely thought to
be relevant to the task of writing posed in English or science classes
. . . Some kind of curriculum coordination—certainly across the
school and possibly across the nation—seems to be indicated.

—Howard Gardner
*Frames of Mind* (192)

A number of years ago I was working with an inner city school in Cleveland, Ohio, providing a series of MI-related professional development workshops ranging from basic to advanced levels of training. In the course of the workshops, the principal of the school got very excited about the Multiple Capacities Wheel. She said to me, "David, this wheel is too important for it to be a hit-or-miss, 'maybe we're doing it, maybe we're not' proposition!" In light of this concern she instituted what I have come to call the Schoolwide Focus model of integrating MI into the curriculum. This model can be adapted to a grade-wide focus or a department-wide focus in the secondary years.

## Purpose of the Schoolwide Focus Model

The purpose of the Schoolwide Focus model is to provide teachers and students with time to zero in on the development of the full range of capacities for targeted intelligences in a given unit. The assumptions of this approach are twofold:

1. Within a given period (each week of a term in the example cited) it is possible to provide students with significant learning tasks that require them to use, practice, and develop the various intelligence capacities.

2. You can accomplish this practice in and through whatever content you are teaching during the period.

## Goals of the Schoolwide Focus Model

- To provide students with a project-based approach to the curriculum that allows them to explore concepts by using them and presenting them to others

- To provide in-context, real-life applications of concepts that are meaningful and exciting to students

- To provide occasions for teachers to collaborate with one another within a school, across grade levels, and within departments to plan and orchestrate hands-on learning experiences for students

- To give students many opportunities to perform their understanding of the required material and to integrate this understanding into their lives

■ To foster students' understanding of the various capacities of the multiple intelligences

## Development of the Schoolwide Focus Model

In the school mentioned, each week of a given term focused on one of the intelligences. During the week it was the teacher's responsibility to make sure that students had opportunities to practice using the various capacities of the focus intelligence in their learning; the teachers were held accountable for using the capacities in their instruction throughout the week.

Needless to say, when this principal came up with the idea initially, the teachers were up in arms. In fact, had it been allowed, they would have stoned her or burned her at the stake. But, after seven to eight weeks of this "forced integration," teachers were thanking her. The principal told me she was getting a number of comments:

> *"You forced us to tap many of the hidden potentials of students that have never been tapped in school before. We now have a totally different picture of what our students can do."*

> *"In the process of requiring students to use all of their intelligence capacities we are seeing some students succeeding who have never succeeded before, simply because we approached teaching and they approached learning in different ways."*

> *"I wasn't a 'happy camper' when you gave us this assignment, but it has stretched me and my students to new levels of performance and learning that we never would have reached without this challenge."*

## Things about This Model That Excite and Interest Me

■ *It has potential for team building in the staff.* Of all the presented ways to integrate MI into the curriculum, the team-building potential of the Schoolwide Focus model is stronger than any of the others. I believe that part of the reason is that teachers and students all face a common challenge: the incorporation of the target intelligences and their capacities into all of the teaching and learning of a week. When teachers and students work together in the manner suggested by this model, a profound collegiality emerges. The staff and students support and encourage one another, and the model fosters working together.

- *It maximizes the use of staff talents.* In some ways this point is an extension of the previous point. The staff will, almost out of necessity, rely on one another to implement ideas. Since the very expectation of the model is that all will be incorporating the capacities throughout the week, those who feel less confident or skilled in certain areas will seek help from those who feel stronger. In the Ohio example, even the nonprofessional staff got into the act of sharing ideas with teachers and encouraging them to try new things in their classrooms!

As you work with this model you may even discover whole areas of talents in people you never knew about. Or you may find that many of your and your students' capacities have been in various states of latency, just waiting for an opportunity like this to burst out and be noticed!

- *Everyone gets stretched to new levels.* In the implementation of this model, not only will everyone have many opportunities to shine or to use capacities they like and in which they have developed skill, but everyone, teachers and students alike, will have to move beyond their comfort zones to use intelligences that are not as fully developed. I personally believe that this kind of stretching is at the heart of any serious educational endeavor. We have all seen the quotation that states that once a mind is stretched beyond its boundaries, it will never again resume its previous boundaries. This concept applies to our multiple intelligences as well. The stretch is good!

- I must also point out that you should not overstretch or stretch too quickly. Comfort zones are one way the brain protects us from perceived danger, so take them very seriously. Nevertheless, you can see taking small steps beyond your comfort zone as authentic challenges; they can become times of significant growth and transformation.

■ *It deepens students' and teachers' learning.* When students and teachers work together throughout a school, a grade level, or a department to incorporate the intelligences into lessons, projects, learning tasks, and so on, their grasp of the material is generally deepened because finding unusual ways to represent the material requires greater cognitive complexity than if we only present it in one way, usually a favorite way. You can very rapidly move far beyond "The facts, ma'am, nothing but the facts" in your teaching to an understanding of process and dynamics that results in synthesis, integration, and application of the material being dealt with in the course of the unit.

## The Basic Process

This model is probably one of the best for implementing a project- or problem-based approach to teaching and learning. Following are the steps for implementing this approach:

**Step 1** Lay out the weeks of a term or of the time in which you will be working with the model. Articulate your objectives and outcomes for the material you will be covering during the chosen time frame.

**Step 2** Map the flow of the curriculum over the chosen time; that is, what particular concepts will you be teaching on which weeks or days? Be specific.

**Step 3** Assign several intelligences to each week. If you see some natural or obvious fits, go ahead and note these. However, it is not critical to do so. Your goal is to touch on all eight intelligences. The MI capacities will be the major learning-process focus for the period.

**Step 4** Match each capacity of the focus intelligence with the curriculum mapping; that is, ask yourself, where during the time will you employ each of the capacities either in your teaching or in learning tasks you develop for your students? Make sure that somewhere and somehow you include all the capacities.

## Evaluations of the Model

Following are some of my own thoughts about the pluses and minuses of the Schoolwide Focus model. I hope you and your colleagues will engage in a similar evaluation of this model in your department, school, or district to find the approach that is best suited to your situation.

### + + + PLUSES + + +

▶ *Everyone is on the same page.* This model has the potential for promoting a great deal of collegiality within a staff, even though students may be dealing with very different content and may be part of different age groups; nevertheless the entire staff has a single focus, namely, to provide learning opportunities that allow students to exercise their various intelligences.

▶ *Teachers rely on and access one another's gifts.* In some ways this is an extension of the previous point, for in implementing this model, all staff members will be challenged, their own intelligences will be strengthened, and they will all gain a new sense of confidence and a resolve to incorporate the intelligences into the curriculum more consistently. This reliance on one another also lessens the risk teachers feel they are taking.

▶ *All students are challenged to stretch and try new things.* The benefits that apply to teachers apply to students, as well. As students are given opportunities to use all their intelligences, they strengthen many of their underdeveloped intelligences, and they become more comfortable in trying new things. Also, since working with the various capacities is a schoolwide focus, all students are trying new things and are more willing to take risks. All are learning together. All are experimenting with the intelligences—students *and* teachers.

▶ *It offers a systematic, disciplined approach to develop MI capacities.* It also provides an excellent format for ensuring that *all* the capacities of a given intelligence are included, not just the "easy" ones, your favorites, or the ones with which you happen to be comfortable.

### - - - MINUSES - - -

▶ *The approach may not fit with what's being taught in a given week; you may run the risk of trivializing or otherwise distorting the curricular concepts just to incorporate the MI capacities.* Of course I must also point out the danger (or bias) lurking within this point: it is conceivable that some teachers will *never* find a fit between any concepts and their weaker intelligences: "I'm sorry, there's just no way to teach algebra using the naturalist, bodily-kinesthetic, and so on, intelligence." You can avoid both traps by planning well ahead and requiring all staff members to use all the capacities at least once.

▶ *Potential exists for inhibiting teacher creativity or causing undue stress.* Depending on how this model is implemented, many teachers may perceive it as a limit to their creativity or autonomy and become unduly anxious, especially when they are working within the realms of their weaker intelligences. However, this potential diminishes as teachers take such risks together and help one another out.

▶ *Students may feel threatened by having to work for a whole week in their weaker intelligences.* If students have not been sufficiently educated about MI, the prospect of using a weaker intelligence for an entire week could cause them undue anxiety and stress. In the upper grades you may also encounter outright resistance to having to work for an extended period with a given intelligence. Be sure that you educate them about MI well, and that you convince them that you are helping them develop their full intellectual potential rather than seeking to trip them up.

## Schoolwide Focus

# *Elementary*

## State or Provincial History

This example illustrates a way to use the Schoolwide Focus
model to teach a unit on state or provincial history. The inspiration for this unit comes from the Elk Elementary Center in
Charleston, West Virginia. For one month each year, they focus
on Appalachian history. I present a more generic unit so that you
can adapt it to whatever the state or provincial history content
is in your curriculum.

## Academic Objectives and Outcomes

● To learn and understand key geographical areas, climatic conditions, and botanical and wildlife species of the state or province and to identify these features on a map

● To understand the most important, formative events in the state's or province's history to the present moment; to understand how this past has shaped and influenced contemporary realities in the state or province

● To identify key historical state or provincial figures and to understand their role and importance

● To learn about present issues and challenges facing the state or province, key people currently in the news, and the state's or province's unique contributions to the nation

● To identify and explain the meaning of state or provincial symbols such as flag, emblem or seal, and songs, and to gain an appreciation for cultural life, including art, music, literature, and folk dances

The example (pages 157–59) assumes that the whole school is studying the state's or province's history, although in the discussion I present several ways to adapt the unit if it doesn't apply to your situation. Part of what I demonstrate is a way to incorporate MI into teaching any content so that you make it come alive for students; this model allows students to learn and process the material on many levels simultaneously, thus touching every cognitive and affective level of their being. Please study the example before beginning.

## Commentary on the Elementary Schoolwide Focus Model Example

I intend these comments to help you understand the unit as I've presented it, and, more important, to assist you in creating your own units using this model.

■ I present a fairly generic approach to the unit's content to provide a template into which you can plug the specifics of the state or provincial history content in your particular curriculum. Likewise, I have not presented all the areas of a state's or province's history you might cover. My goal was to provide enough to get you started.

■ The example unit assumes that it will be a schoolwide project; however, there are some obvious adaptations that must occur to make the curriculum appropriate for various grade levels. For example, you might use puppets, storytelling, and singing in the early grades to study historical figures and events. Some learning could occur by asking children in the upper grades to create a series of mini-dramas for the younger children.

■ Note that I do not incorporate all of the capacities of the intelligences that would be used during the various weeks. I use several intelligences each week, and by the end of the month, all the intelligences were used, albeit with a stronger emphasis on some than on others. In the next unit, I would emphasize those intelligences I did not use much in this unit. Using the MI Capacities Wheels (pages 19 and 20) to design units ensures that, by the end of a term, you will have incorporated all the capacities of the various intelligences into the curriculum.

Another way to design this unit is to focus for a whole week on one intelligence, making sure to use all of the capacities of the target intelligence and to match the capacities to the content. For example, if the content for a week were key natural features and the target intelligence is visual-spatial, you might have a week that incorporates the following capacities in the following ways:

➤ Active imagination—*Study pictures of some of the state's or province's most interesting land formations and see what you find in them.*

➤ Forming mental images—*Visualize yourself as a bird flying over the state or province, or as a mouse on the ground, and note what you see.*

➤ Graphic representation—*Create a picture book or montage that illustrates land formations, water, plants, and animals.*

➤ Finding your way in space—*Create games that develop state or province map-reading skills.*

➤ Accurate perception from various angles—*Study various perspectives on the state or province, for example, from the ground, air, or space.*

➤ Image manipulations—*Play with the image of the state or province and see what you can make using its shape.*

➤ Recognizing relationships between objects—*Study geographical formations and how they were formed by natural objects or phenomena.*

I don't feel there is one right way to use this model. I simply present an example, then explore other ways it can be used. The key is to find the approach that makes the most sense, both in terms of the content you are teaching and in terms of your comfort in using this model.

■ Although in the unit as I've presented it, the culmination is the week-long, schoolwide celebration of the state, there are a number of other possible culminating events that come to mind: a presentation for parents; a grade-level presentation for the other grades; a videotaped show to present to other schools; and so on.

■ As you consider using this model, consider adopting one of a number of other schoolwide themes you could easily plug into this framework: seasonal celebrations, national holidays, special days on the calendar, and so on. In each case you work with the model in the same manner as I have outlined above.

# Schoolwide Focus Model for Elementary School

## State or Provincial History Month

### Objectives and Outcomes
**What are the key concepts and skills to be addressed?**

Students will understand the history of their state or province, including the part played by key figures, formative events, symbols, cultures, geography, population, and so on. They will present their learning in a week-long culminating celebration (see page 159 for more detail).

### Room Needs
**What are the various spaces and areas required?**

- tables for student art projects
- space to store products created for use in the celebration
- hallway areas for displays of student-created works

### Resources
**What materials, equipment, speakers, videos, and so on are needed?**

- posters, brochures, pamphlets, and other tourist information about the state or province
- art supplies including paints, marking pens, colored chalk
- scheduled field trips and speakers
- filmstrips, audiocassettes, videocassettes about the state or province
- historical and contemporary research materials

### Assessment
**What multimodal ways will you use to evaluate the learning?**

The students stand around a large map of the state or province they created. Ask various students to explain or review items on the map. Give students each a blank map of the state or province and ask them to show individually, *in any way they choose*, their understanding of five key figures, five key events, five key geographical features, and five current statistics.

# Schoolwide Focus Model for Elementary School
## State or Provincial History Month

| | Monday | Tuesday | Wednesday | Thursday | Friday |
|---|---|---|---|---|---|
| **Week 1**<br><br>*Content Focus*<br>Geography, Environment, and Population<br><br>*Intelligence Focus*<br>Visual-Spatial<br>Logical-Mathematical<br>Naturalist<br>Verbal-Linguistic<br>Bodily-Kinesthetic | Show students a movie or filmstrip about the state or province. Discuss it. (V-L)<br><br>Students make a very large map of the state. Throughout the month, they will use the map to record, display, and otherwise show the information they learn about the state or province. (V-S) | Students find out some facts and figures related to the state or province, such as population, population centers, climate throughout the year, geography, vegetation, wildlife, natural resources, and so on. They graph the information. (L-M) | Students find appropriate visual ways to show on the large state map information they have found in their research. For example, they may add mountains with clay, color-code various types of vegetation. (V-S, B-K)<br><br>Using posters, travel and sight-seeing brochures, magazines, and so on, students make a montage or some kind of display that shows things they find most interesting or exciting about their state or province. (V-S) | Take students on a nature field trip or a trip to a state museum to show them the state or province flower, bird, geographical features, vegetation, and so on. Include some state or province history. You will build on this information in the following weeks. (V-L, NAT) | Students make new additions to the large state or province map based on the previous week's learning. (V-S) |
| **Week 2**<br><br>*Content Focus*<br>Key People and Events<br><br>*Intelligence Focus*<br>Verbal-Linguistic<br>Interpersonal<br>Bodily-Kinesthetic<br>Visual-Spatial | In cooperative, expert groups, students jigsaw written material about key historical figures and events that shaped the state's or province's history. Each student takes a topic to research, then they come together to put all the pieces together. (V-L, INTER) | In groups, students create reports on key figures or events to go into a class booklet on the state or province. (V-L) | Students make up a set of games to communicate their research findings to the rest of the class. (V-L, INTER) | Students play key historical event charades. (B-K)<br><br>Students create a role-play to communicate information about historical figures. (B-K) | Students make up a guessing game based on key figures and events, much like *What's My Line?* (V-L) |

# Schoolwide Focus Model for Elementary School
## State or Provincial History Month

| | Monday | Tuesday | Wednesday | Thursday | Friday |
|---|---|---|---|---|---|
| **Week 3**<br><u>*Content Focus*</u><br>Symbols, Mythology, and Culture<br><br><u>*Intelligence Focus*</u><br>Visual-Spatial<br>Intrapersonal<br>Auditory-Vibrational<br>Bodily-Kinesthetic<br>Interpersonal<br>Verbal-Linguistic | Students learn the state or province song and discuss its meaning and significance to individuals. (A-V, V-L, INTRA)<br><br>Students study the state or province flag and discuss its meaning and significance to individuals. (V-S, V-L, INTRA)<br><br>Students study the state or province seal or emblem and discuss its meaning and significance to individuals. (V-S, INTRA).<br><br>Students study and learn folk dances from the state or province and ways they are related to the life of the people who live there. (B-K, A-V) | As a class, students study the state's or province's cultures and subcultures and the contributions of some key artists, songwriters, poets, storytellers, and so on. Which do they like most and why? (INTER) | Students write a new state or province song that includes information they have learned. (A-V)<br><br>Students create an original, creative dance to express the greatness of the state or province and the history that brought it to its present. (B-K, A-V) | Students create a new flag or emblem that symbolizes some of the more important things they learned. (V-S) | Students reflect in some type of journal on the reasons they like the state or province and what they can do to make it better. (V-L, INTRA) |
| **Week 4**<br><u>*Content Focus*</u><br>A Celebration of Our State or Province<br><br><u>*Intelligence Focus*</u><br>All Eight | Throughout the week, the entire school participates in a celebration of the state or province. Obviously, the celebration will involve all intelligences and capacities students have been using and developing throughout the unit. Following are some suggestions for the celebration:<br><br>■ Use the products from the previous three weeks (the large state or province map that shows various factual information, the new flags and seals) to decorate the hallways of the school.<br><br>■ Ask students to sing the state or province song and share the new songs they have created.<br><br>■ Ask students to teach one another (maybe across grade levels) the dances they have created to express the story of and their pride in their state or province.<br><br>■ Hold some of the celebration outdoors in some great natural environment unique to the state or province. | | | | |

# Middle School

## Statistics and Probability

This example illustrates a grade-level adaptation of the Schoolwide Focus model to teach a unit on statistics and probability to eighth graders. In the example, students work with a variety of situations that they find meaningful.

## Academic Objectives and Outcomes

- To learn the proper procedures for gathering and recording data for use in compiling meaningful statistics and the basic math operations needed, such as working with fractions and decimals, averaging, tallying

- To understand how to graph research data, how to interpret the graphed data, and how to explain its significance and meaning to another, including implications of the data

- To understand the process of deriving statistics from gathered and graphed data and to demonstrate the process for another person using items from daily life

- To understand the process of making predictions based on carefully analyzed statistics and to demonstrate the process for another using items from one's daily life

- To explain, interpret, and defend one's predictions

At the heart of this example (pages 165–68) is a problem-based approach to instruction. You're not concerned with right answers as much as you are with the students' understanding of tallying, graphing, probability, hypothesizing, finding and comparing fractions and decimals, averaging, and working with statistics. By using all intelligences to teach concepts that are basically logical-mathematical, you will reach more students and get more understanding than if you were to teach in only a logical-mathematical manner. Please study the example before beginning.

The inspiration for this unit came from a wonderful book by Mark Wahl entitled *Math for Humans: Teaching Math through Seven Intelligences.*

## Commentary on the Middle School Grade-Level Focus Model Example

Although I have called this model the Schoolwide Focus model, the fundamental insight of the model is not limited to a whole school. In the secondary years, you can use this model to focus a department, or in the case of the unit I have presented here, to focus a grade level.

■ As you look over this unit, remember that my goal is to demonstrate ways to integrate MI into content that is often part of middle school math curriculum. I am *not* making content suggestions. I *am* suggesting, however, that it is possible to do what I have done in this example with *any* unit.

■ While you can also apply the model within a single class rather than across a grade level, as I have suggested here, part of the power of this model is that all students in a given grade are having the same experience. Also, as teachers share ideas, a certain synergy occurs. You'll probably find that you have a much better unit than any one individual could have designed alone! And what is more, you may even make new discoveries about the very material you have probably taught many times, simply because you are exploring the concepts using all of your intelligences, as well.

■ Throughout the example I point out the various intelligences and the capacities involved in the learning tasks. This approach is somewhat artificial, because in normal people, all intelligences work together in fairly well orchestrated ways, albeit with some intelligences being stronger than others. Nevertheless, the various intelligences overlap and collaborate. In fact one could make a strong case that, in some ways, all intelligences are involved in almost everything we do.

Given my comments I still want you to be able to analyze this example, and I want to demonstrate ways you can focus student learning and your instruction on several intelligences by very intentionally planning learning tasks around the MI capacities. In the process, not only will students learn the material better (they'll know it in at least eight ways!), they will also get to know their own multiple intelligences. As I mentioned earlier in this book, in some ways the intelligences are like any skill that we have developed in our lives—the more we practice them and use them, the more comfortable we become at using them and the more skilled we become. Use of this model is analogous to going to the MI gym for an intelligence aerobic workout!

■ Some experiments in the third week suggest that students gather data and make predictions based on the normal life of the school. At first glance, this task may seem impossible, for students are in class at the very times they are supposed to be gathering the initial data and testing their predictions. However, many of the observation activities can be assigned as homework, only it is to be done during the school day as opposed to at home after school. Students can gather data before school starts, between classes, during lunch, and after school. Talk with participating teachers to figure out the logistics for this observation and data gathering.

■ You can handle the culmination fair in week 4 in a number of ways, including a special display area that students visit during lunch or before or after school, as an evening event to which the community and parents are invited, or as a traveling road show that students take to other classes in the school. Again, let the creativity of your fellow teachers be the guide on what to do for the culminating event. What you are after is a way for students to use the information of the unit in as close to a real-life situation as possible, and you want them to explain and demonstrate for others the concepts they have learned. When they have to perform their understanding, the learning tends to be cemented and deepened.

■ When working with a grade-level curricular focus, as much as possible find ways to integrate all the learning from the various subjects into themes or interdisciplinary explorations. In this case, you would simply pull the content for your subject area through the theme or interdisciplinary focal point, basically teaching what you were going to teach anyway. When you look at themes, it makes everyone's work easier and also tends to create a story line for what you are teaching and what students are learning.

■ If I were going to create a truly interdisciplinary exploration of statistics and probability it might look as follows:

➤ Language arts—Learn the appropriate vocabulary related to statistics and probability, read about statistics and probability, make predictions about what will happen in a story based on a statistical analysis of data from the story, write reports on your findings from the prediction activities in which you have engaged

➤ Mathematics—Learn the various processes and operations necessary to work with statistics and probability such as averaging, converting fractions to decimals, graphing

➤ Science—Predict what will happen in an experiment, defending your prediction based on a careful analysis of data; do the experiment to test your predictions; evaluate and reflect on your prediction ability.

➤ Social studies and history—Study various cultures and periods of history. What perspectives on prediction and probability did the culture hold? What role does prediction play in the culture or historical era?

➤ Fine arts—Listen to several pieces of music and tally the occurrence of certain musical or rhythmic patterns in the music, then listen to still another piece seeing if you can predict where the music will go next.

■ A comment I made when reflecting on the elementary example bears repeating here. What I have done in this example is a little bit fake, for you really can't isolate the intelligences as I have done; they tend to work in a fairly integrated fashion within each of us. However, the point I make is that you can definitely place emphasis on certain intelligences and their capacities to the exclusion of others; however, by hook or by crook, all of the intelligences will likely find their way into the unit in one form or another. Your job in working with this model is to keep the cognitive focus on the capacities of the intelligences with which you are dealing during a given week; don't worry about other intelligences that may appear.

# Grade-Level Focus Model for Middle School

## A Statistics, Prediction, and Probability Fair

### Objectives and Outcomes
What are the key concepts and skills to be addressed?

Students will learn how to gather, tally, and graph data, how to do statistical analysis based on the data, and how to make and test predictions. They will demonstrate and explain their learning to classmates in a culminating statistics and probability fair (see page 168 for more details).

### Room Needs
What are the various spaces and areas required?

- space for group work
- space to store the project work for the fair
- areas of school students will need to use to gather the necessary data

### Resources
What materials, equipment, speakers, videos, and so on are needed?

- graph paper, rulers, protractors, and so on
- art supplies, including marking pens, colored chalk
- variety of magazines to cut up
- audiocassette recorder
- jelly beans and M&Ms
- dice and spinners from board games

### Assessment
What multimodal ways will you use to evaluate the learning?

At the end of each week, students will demonstrate their understanding of the concepts covered in the week through various application projects. In the final week, their work will be assessed in and through the presentation at the fair and their explanations and applications of the concepts covered in the unit.

# Grade-Level Focus Model for Middle School
## A Statistics, Prediction, and Probability Fair

**Week 1**

*Content Focus*
Predicting from Counts and Graphs

*Intelligence Focus*
Verbal–Linguistic
Visual–Spatial
Logical–Mathematical
Interpersonal
Intrapersonal
Auditory–Vibrational

| | Monday | Tuesday | Wednesday | Thursday | Friday |
|---|---|---|---|---|---|
| | Students learn the appropriate vocabulary for the unit (for example, data, sample average, statistics, prediction). (V-L) | Pairs create a bar graph that compares the words most frequently used in the advertisements to those least used. (L-M) | Based on their graphs of the word counts, students predict which words will occur most often in other written advertisements of the product they have chosen. (L-M, V-L) | Students discuss the similarities and differences between printed advertisements and those on television. (V-S, L-M, V-L) | Students review the concepts and learning of the week, including asking questions they may have. (INTRA) |
| | Students work in pairs to cut out ten advertisements from magazines that deal with the same type of product (for example, a car) and make a collage. (V-S) | Pairs predict which words will show up in the advertisements other students analyze. (L-M, INTER) | Students test their predictions by repeating the same process with ten additional advertisements of their product in different magazines from those they used the first time. (L-M, V-L) | Students use their graphs to predict how many of the words used frequently in the magazine advertisements will be used in radio and TV advertisements. They give reasons for their predictions. (L-M, V-L) | Application project for the fair. Students submit class plans for ways to duplicate the counting, graphing, and predicting exercises they did during the week. They may use something that interests them, such as tennis shoes, favorite foods, favorite TV shows, and so on. (INTER, V-L, A-V, V-S) |
| | Using colored markers, students go through the advertisements and color-code repeating words—a new color for each word that is repeated. (V-L, V-S) | Pairs share their findings with other pairs to test their predictions. (L-M, INTER) | Again, students count and color-code the words, make a graph, and analyze the results. (L-M, V-S) | Students play the tapes of the radio and TV advertisements, counting and graphing repeated words. (L-M, V-L, A-V) | Students compare results to the predictions. (L-M) |
| | As homework, partners create an audiocassette of ten radio and ten TV advertisements of the same type of product they used in their montage. They will use the tapes in the culminating fair. (A-V, V-S) | | | | |

# Grade-Level Focus Model for Middle School
## A Statistics, Prediction, and Probability Fair

| | Monday | Tuesday | Wednesday | Thursday | Friday |
|---|---|---|---|---|---|
| **Week 2**<br><br>*Content Focus*<br>Predicting from Fractions and Decimals<br><br><br>*Intelligence Focus*<br>Logical-Mathematical<br>Interpersonal<br>Visual-Spatial<br>Verbal-Linguistic | Students work in teams of three to four. Give each team a bag of jelly beans. Students count the jelly beans, then count the individual colors. (L-M, V-S, INTER)<br><br>Students figure out the fraction of all the jelly beans that each color comprises (L-M)<br><br>Students convert each fraction to a decimal. (L-M) | Students play a prediction game. They pour a bag of jelly beans out on a table. They **predict** how many times out of forty (a fraction or decimal) a blindfolded person will select a red jelly bean from the mass. Blindfold one person, mix the jelly beans, and ask the blindfolded person to select one. The team records the color. They put the bean back, mix, and repeat forty times. They calculate the fraction of times a red jelly bean was selected. (L-M) | Students repeat the prediction game using M&Ms instead of jelly beans. (L-M)<br><br>Students analyze their original predictions from Tuesday. Do the results of the game match the predictions? (L-M)<br><br>Teams discuss the prediction game, listing possible reasons for the similarities and differences in their predictions and the actual outcomes. (V-L, INTER) | Teams make up another prediction game based on analyzing statistics, probability, and testing and understanding the results of the game. (INTER, L-M)<br><br>Teams try out their games on one another and discuss the results of the various experiences. (V-L, INTER)<br><br>Students play a game of chance. They predict how many of eighty throws of dice or spins of a spinner will come up odd and how many even. They roll three dice or spin a spinner at least eighty times. Then they graph the results, stating the probability in fractions. (L-M, V-L) | Students review the concepts and learning from the week, including their questions. (V-L)<br><br>Application project for the fair: Students design a public opinion poll based on their work analyzing statistics, making predictions, and so on. (INTER, V-L, L-M) |

# Grade-Level Focus Model for Middle School
## A Statistics, Prediction, and Probability Fair

| | Monday | Tuesday | Wednesday | Thursday | Friday |
|---|---|---|---|---|---|
| **Week 3**<br><br>_Content Focus_<br>Statistics and Predictions in Daily Life<br><br>_Intelligence Focus_<br>Logical-Mathematical<br>Interpersonal<br>Visual-Spatial<br>Bodily-Kinesthetic<br>Verbal-Linguistic<br>Intrapersonal | Help the class design a tally sheet to gather statistics on characteristics of classmates (for example, hair color, glasses, height, types of shoes and other clothing) in the various grade levels. (L-M)<br><br>During the remainder of the day, students gather information to fill in the tally sheet; they will use the information during the rest of the week. (V-S, L-M) | Students use a bar graph to show the results of the survey taken Monday. (L-M, V-S)<br><br>Students compute various statistics based on the data: the average numbers of males and females who wore an article of clothing, the percentage of students in each grade who wore the same kind of clothes, the average height of students in each grade. (L-M) | Using the graph from Tuesday and the data compiled from it, students make predictions about the people they saw on Wednesday. They give themselves one point for each accurate prediction of the second ten people. (V-S, L-M)<br><br>Students create an observation chart to mark off the character-istics they see. (V-S, L-M)<br><br>Students go with a partner to the chosen spot and observe; one partner is the observer, one is the recorder. (V-S, V-L, INTER) | Students give themselves five points for every accurate prediction they made about the first ten people they saw. They give themselves one point for each accurate prediction of the second ten people. (V-S, L-M)<br><br>Students share their results with their teammates and discuss why their scores were high or low. As a class, students brainstorm steps that can help them make more accurate predictions. (INTER, L-M) | Application project for the fair: Students make and submit to you plans for reporting their data, statistics, and predictions for the week to their classmates and other classes at the fair. (V-L, V-S)<br><br>Students review the concepts and learning from the week, including their questions. (V-L, INTRA) |

Throughout this week, students create a miniature fair for the rest of the school, with booths to visit. All the booths must be adaptations of the statistics, predictions, and probability work students have been doing throughout the three weeks. Obviously, the process of creating and conducting the fair will involve all the intelligences and the capacities students have been using and developing throughout the unit. Following are some suggestions for the fair:

| **Week 4**<br><br>_Content Focus_<br>Analyzing and Prediction from Data in Everyday Life<br><br>_Intelligence Focus_<br>All Eight | | | | | |
|---|---|---|---|---|---|

- Set up a series of games of chance (dice, spinners, cards, and so on). Students figure out the odds of winning ahead of time, then see if participants can beat the odds.
- Students set up a display based on the work they did in weeks 1 and 2. Some of the information they will simply share with others, but as much as possible, they will ask visitors to repeat some of the experiments, such as the ones with jelly beans and M&Ms. Students make up some new prediction games to try out on visitors.
- Students set up a "Getting to Know Your School" booth. Students ask visitors to predict some of the same things they did in week 3, then share the results of their experiments.

## The Living Cell

This example illustrates a department adaptation of the School-wide Focus model to teach a high school unit on the living cell. Special thanks is due to Lee Mastrodonato, a good friend and a colleague in the task of making learning meaningful and exciting for his students; I appreciate his consultation, critique, and assistance in helping me put together this example. Lee is a science teacher at Nightingale Middle School in Chicago, Illinois. A visit to his website at http://www.geocities.com/Athens/Troy/3908/ is definitely worth your while!

## Academic Objectives and Outcomes

- To learn and understand the fundamental structure common to most living cells including vacuoles, membranes, mitochondria, ribosomes, and cytoplasm, and the unique function of each part

- To identify the parts of the cell under a microscope and to understand some of the key facts, figures, and statistics about their various functions

- To understand the life processes of the cell, including such things as excretion, respiration, reproduction, mitosis, active and passive transport, electrical transmission (nerve and cardiac cells), chemical manufacture (T-cells, Goblet cells), phagocytosis, transport (red blood cells), movement (muscle cells, cardiac cells), and so on

- To identify various kinds of cells and to understand their specialized functions; for example, why do plant cells have cell walls in addition to cell membranes? Why do nerve cells have insulation around parts of them?

- To understand the role of the cell as an individual, but also its role as part of a greater whole, moving from the individual cell to its relationships with surrounding cells to its importance to organs of which it is a part to the whole body system to the body in its social relationships and beyond

- To understand ways to care for cells and maintain optimal cell health

While this example is very content-specific, I ask you to think of ways you could plug your content into the various learning tasks and activities as you study the example. My goal is to demonstrate ways multiple intelligences can help us increase students' motivation for learning, ways they can make the learning more meaningful by helping students make more connections between their own lives and their schooling, and ways MI aids us in more accurately assessing the learning that is actually taking place in our classrooms—learning that often eludes us in a purely verbal-linguistic or logical-mathematical approach.

Many high school teachers who have integrated MI into their curriculum note that more students get involved with the material and succeed more often; teachers understand what students understand; and students have more say about their own learning and what will help them, especially if the teachers are regularly teaching *about* multiple intelligences as part of their regular instruction. Please study the example (pages 173–78) before beginning.

## Commentary on the High School Departmentwide Focus Model Example

As I noted in the commentary on the middle school example, effective use of this model is not limited to a whole school. In the secondary years (middle and high school) this model could be called the "Grade-Level Focus" model, or in the case of the unit I have presented here, the "Departmentwide Focus" model.

Following are a number of observations on this example. These comments are intended to help you understand the unit, and, more important, to help you create your own units using this model.

- Depending on your curriculum, you may or may not take a month to teach the material. This model is not time-specific.

- Many of the comments about the middle school example apply here, as well, so please review them.

- The suggestion of the children's museum project as a culminating event is but one way to ask students to represent their understanding in a variety of ways. To take these (or any!) concepts and present them in a way that young children can grasp requires a fairly thorough understanding of the material. Students are instantly catapulted to the higher-order thinking levels of Bloom's now-famous taxonomy.

  While I do not think that the children's museum idea is vital or even the best idea, its purpose as a culminating event is to force students to apply their learning to real life situations. Some educational literature refers to this approach as *constructivist* because students must create their own meaning. In some ways it is also in line with what others are calling "problem-based learning."

■ While the example here assumes a block or intensive schedule, I do not believe that the use of this model is limited in that way. If you have the more traditional forty- to fifty-minute periods, simply narrow the learning tasks to what your students can complete within that time frame. You may deal only with one intelligence per day, and the learning tasks related to a particular intelligence may extend over several days.

■ As in the other examples, I am not making content suggestions; what I am suggesting is that, as a department, you do some common planning so that, regardless of the content you'll be teaching, the whole department would be working with similar learning tasks and activities. You'll need to adjust and align the curriculum to make sense, in other words, so that across the department you are teaching comparable concepts at the same time, or concepts that fit into a common template. In this example, the same learning tasks could be applied with equal effectiveness in chemistry and in earth science.

■ I do not believe you will be able to use the department-wide focus model to teach everything during the term. However, with some planning at the beginning of a term, you will likely be able to find a number of concepts you'll be covering that can be taught in the manner I'm suggesting.

# Departmentwide Focus Model for High School

## Biology: The Living Cell Museum

### Objectives and Outcomes
*What are the key concepts and skills to be addressed?*

Students will understand the basic structure and life process common to most cells; they will be able to identify the parts and functions of a cell, as well as various kinds of cells and their specialized functions. They will present their learning and discoveries to others in a culminating museum display (see page 177 for more details).

### Room Needs
*What are the various spaces and areas required?*

- arrangement for cooperative group work
- space for students' projects and for storing works in progress
- a place for displaying the museum exhibits

### Resources
*What materials, equipment, speakers, videos, and so on are needed?*

- appropriate science videos or filmstrips that deal with parts and functions of a cell
- art supplies, including paints, marking pens, colored chalk, and clay
- appropriate lab materials and supplies, for example, microscopes, varieties of cell tissue samples
- necessary written information
- computers, modems, and Internet access
- audiocassette recorders and blank tapes

### Assessment
*What multimodal ways will you use to evaluate the learning?*

Throughout each week, students will demonstrate their understanding in a variety of performances: role-plays, written work, three-dimensional models, labs, and so on. The projects require students to pull together the learning of the week in new forms that people outside the class would understand and be interested in. Talk to and ask students about their museum displays to determine what they got out of the material.

# Departmentwide Focus Model for High School
## Biology: The Living Cell Museum

| Week 1 | Monday | Tuesday | Wednesday | Thursday | Friday |
|---|---|---|---|---|---|
| **Content Focus**<br>Cell Structure (parts, location, and functions)<br><br>**Intelligence Focus**<br>Visual-Spatial<br>Logical-Mathematical<br>Verbal-Linguistic<br>Auditory-Vibrational<br>Interpersonal<br>Intrapersonal | Show a video on the parts of a cell and their functions. (V-S) | Lab: Students observe cells under the microscope and locate the parts they studied. (V-S) | In teams, students research facts and figures about cell parts, that is, size, weight, and so on. They use the Internet, if possible. (INTER, L-M, V-L) | Students create a series of analogies to help them understand the facts and figures they have uncovered. For example, how many cells laid end-to-end would it take to equal their height? How many cells would it take to fill a soda bottle? (V-L, L-M) | Project: Students take all they have learned about the parts, locations, and functions of a cell and create a children's museum display to teach younger students about cells. (INTER, V-S, L-M, V-L) |
| | As teams, students study formal definitions of each part of the cell and its function, including vacuoles, membranes, mitochondria, ribosomes, and so on. They write definitions using their own language. (V-L, INTER) | Students sketch what they observe, labeling the parts and adding to the drawings as appropriate. (V-S, V-L) | Students use their research to make three-dimensional models of a cell, appropriately labeling each part. (V-S, V-L, INTER) | Students create a musical audiocassette that includes a theme song for each cell part. They explain why and how the song reflects the workings of a cell. (A-V, V-L) | Students record their reflections on the week's learning and discoveries in a journal or learning diary. (INTRA) |
| | Teams divide the cell parts among their members. Each student creates a web of the assigned part using own notes and research. (V-S, INTRA, L-M) | Student share their sketches with several other students, noting the similarities and differences between their drawings. (V-S, INTER, L-M) | | | |

# Departmentwide Focus Model for High School
## Biology: The Living Cell Museum

| | Monday | Tuesday | Wednesday | Thursday | Friday |
|---|---|---|---|---|---|
| **Week 2**<br><br>*Content Focus*<br>Various Kinds of Cells and Their Elements<br><br>*Intelligence Focus*<br>Visual-Spatial<br>Bodily-Kinesthetic<br>Logical-Mathematical<br>Verbal-Linguistic<br>Interpersonal<br>Intrapersonal | Lab work: Students use a microscope to observe the various kinds of cells such as plant cells, blood cells, muscle cells, and so on. (V-S)<br><br>Students use appropriate colors, shapes, and designs to sketch the various kinds of cells they observe. (V-S)<br><br>Students create a series of Venn diagrams and record the similarities and differences they observe in the cells. (V-S, L-M, V-L) | Students read about specific elements of various kinds of cells that allow them to function. (V-L)<br><br>Students create a matrix by listing cells across the top and their functions down the side. They fill in the intersections with information they have been learning. (L-M, V-L) | Divide the class into two groups, plant and animal. Each group creates an advertisement for their cell, including appropriate visual aids and text. (V-L, V-S, INTER)<br><br>The cell teams use as much of their information as possible to write a script for Wednesday's advertisement and questions for Thursday's press conference. (V-L, INTER) | Each cell group presents its advertisement to the rest of the class, who act as reporters at a press conference and ask appropriate questions concerning the inter-dynamics of the cell. (V-L, V-S)<br><br>Project: Students take all they have learned about the parts, locations, and functions of a cell and create a children's museum display to teach younger students about cells. (INTER, V-S, V-L, L-M) | Students record their reflections on the week's learning and discoveries in a journal or learning diary. (INTRA) |

# Departmentwide Focus Model for High School

## Biology: The Living Cell Museum

| Week 3 / Content Focus / Intelligence Focus | Monday | Tuesday | Wednesday | Thursday | Friday |
|---|---|---|---|---|---|
| **Week 3** *Content Focus* Cell Life Processes | | | | | |
| *Intelligence Focus* | | | | | |
| Verbal-Linguistic | In teams, students find definitions for the following words: excretion / respiration / mitosis / reproduction / transport / active and passive / electrical transmission (nerve and cardiac cells) / chemical manufacture (T- cells, goblet cells) / phagocytosis / transport (red blood cells) (V-L, INTER) | Students review the processes they studied Monday by writing their own definitions for each process in their own language: they share the definitions with partners, giving helpful feedback. (INTER, V-L) | Students write a short story called "A Day in the Life of a Cell." (V-L) | | |
| Logical-Mathematical | | With partners, students draw as many analogies as they can between a human's day and that of a cell.(L-M, V-L) | | | |
| Visual-Spatial | | | Students create a cartoon series that illustrates the story they have written. (INTER, V-S) | After each show the teams share their cartoons. (INTER, V-S) | Project: Students take all they have learned about the parts, locations, and functions of a cell and create a children's museum display to teach younger students about cells. (INTER, V-S, V-L, L-M) |
| Bodily-Kinesthetic | | | | | |
| Interpersonal | | | | Class discussion: Ask students what they found most interesting. What questions do they still have about cells? (V-L, INTER, INTRA) | |
| Intrapersonal | | | Students prepare their stories as radio shows in which they include appropriate sound effects, musical interludes, and so on. (A-V) | Each group presents its radio show to the class. (INTER, A-V) | Students record their reflections on the week's learning and discoveries in a journal or learning diary. (INTRA) |
| Auditory-Vibrational | | | | | |

# Departmentwide Focus Model for High School

## Biology: The Living Cell Museum

| | Monday | Tuesday | Wednesday | Thursday | Friday |
|---|---|---|---|---|---|
| **Week 4**<br><br>_Content Focus_<br>**The Roles of the Cell as an Individual Part and as Part of a Larger Whole**<br><br>_Intelligence Focus_<br>**All Eight** | Students study the concept of the individual cell as it relates to a whole organism, including cell-to-cell, cell-to-organ, and organ-to-body interactions. (NAT)<br><br>Lab: Students observe various kinds of cells in relation to their immediate neighboring cells and in relation to all the cells in the "neighborhood." They record all the relationships. (L-M, NAT, V-L) | Cell National Assembly Dramatization<br>Divide students into various groups to study key cells in the human body. Students imagine the body is a nation and the cells are its citizens. Each cell group is to perform the following tasks.<br><br>Students research and discuss the role of their cell group in the body-nation; for example, are they the legislative, executive, or judicial branch? Are they a lobby group? On what other cell group do they most rely? (INTER, L-M)<br><br>Students use the Internet to help them understand the role of their cell group as an individual group and as part of a larger cell group. Check out these websites:<br>http://www.cellsalive.com/<br>http://www.chem4kids.com/<br>http://www.biology4kids/key/map.html<br>http://www.eurekascience.com/ICanDoThat/bacteria_cells.htm<br>http://www.dcn.davis.ca.us | Students make flowcharts that show where they fit into the governing process of the body-nation. (V-S, L-M, INTER)<br><br>Students share charts with the class. As a class, they discuss the kind of government the body-nation has. (INTER, V-L) | Students set up a mock town meeting to deal with a problem the body-nation is facing. Each cell group plays its role in the meeting. Following are suggestions:<br><br>• A virus has just entered the body. What do we need to do?<br><br>• The body is not getting a balanced diet. How is poor diet affecting us?<br><br>• Discuss what must be part of a "Cell's Bill of Rights." What do cells need to operate most effectively?<br><br>• The body is abusing us with alcohol or drugs. What are the results and what can we do about it? (B-K, V-L, L-M, INTER) | Project work: Students create a display for the museum that starts with one cell, then adds one to make two, then adds more to become an organ; the organs, a body; the body, a family, society, and so on. (V-S, L-M)<br><br>Students record their reflections on the week's learning and discoveries in a journal or learning diary. (INTRA, V-L)<br><br>Pull together the project work from the month as a way to review your learning about the living cell. Set up a display area and invite other classmates and classes to visit. (All Eight) |

# Schoolwide, Grade-Level, or Departmentwide Focus Work Sheet

## Unit Name _____

### Objectives and Outcomes
What are the key concepts and skills to be addressed?

### Room Needs
What are the various spaces and areas required?

### Resources
What materials, equipment, speakers, videos, and so on are needed?

### Assessment
What multimodal ways will you use to evaluate the learning?

# Schoolwide, Grade-Level, or Departmentwide Focus Work Sheet

State a theme and an appropriate intelligence focus for each week, then work the content and capacities across the days of the week.

| | Monday | Tuesday | Wednesday | Thursday | Friday |
|---|---|---|---|---|---|
| Week 1<br><br>*Intelligence Focus* | | | | | |

# Schoolwide, Grade-Level, or Departmentwide Focus Work Sheet

State a theme and an appropriate intelligence focus for each week, then work the content and capacities across the days of the week.

| | Monday | Tuesday | Wednesday | Thursday | Friday |
|---|---|---|---|---|---|
| Week 2<br><br>*Intelligence Focus* | | | | | |

# Schoolwide, Grade-Level, or Departmentwide Focus Work Sheet

State a theme and an appropriate intelligence focus for each week, then work the content and capacities across the days of the week.

| | Monday | Tuesday | Wednesday | Thursday | Friday |
|---|---|---|---|---|---|
| Week 3<br><br>_Intelligence Focus_ | | | | | |

# Schoolwide, Grade-Level, or Departmentwide Focus Work Sheet

State a theme and an appropriate intelligence focus for each week, then work the content and capacities across the days of the week.

| Week 4 / Intelligence Focus | Monday | Tuesday | Wednesday | Thursday | Friday |
|---|---|---|---|---|---|
|  |  |  |  |  |  |

# Schoolwide Reflection Log

### Other units I could apply this model to:

### Modifications I would make to this model:

### Things I particularly like about this model:

### The biggest challenges I anticipate in using this model:

# 7

# Some Restructuring Implications of the Theory

**MI**

*Without a doubt, one of the reasons that MI theory has attracted attention in the educational community is because of its ringing endorsement of an ensemble of propositions: we are not all the same; we do not all have the same kinds of minds; education works most effectively for most individuals if these differences in mentation and strengths are taken into account rather than denied or ignored. I have always believed that the heart of the MI perspective—in theory and in practice—inheres in taking human differences seriously.*

—Howard Gardner
"Reflections on Multiple Intelligences: Myths and Messages" (208)

I believe that the cutting edge of multiple intelligence research is the wide variety of practical implementations of the theory that are currently under way in hundreds of schools, school districts, and school divisions around the world. This book is primarily about one aspect of this implementation, integrating multiple intelligences into the existing curriculum. In some ways, when you touch the curriculum of a school, you touch its heart. Any changes to the curriculum send ripples across every aspect of the school, much like a stone thrown into the proverbial calm pond. In this final chapter I revisit some of the research on which this book is based and reiterate some of the conclusions about implementation I have drawn from the research. However, a caution from Howard Gardner (1998) is very much in order before I continue:

> **MI theory is in no way an educational prescription. There is always a gulf between psychological claims about how the mind works and educational practices, and such a gulf is especially apparent in a theory that was developed without specific educational goals in mind. Thus, in educational discussions, I have always taken the position that educators are in the best position to determine the uses to which MI theory can and should be put . . .**
>
> **I have tried to encourage certain "applied MI efforts," but in general my advice has echoed the traditional Chinese adage, "Let a hundred flowers blossom." And I have often been surprised and delighted by the fragrance of some of these fledgling plants.(206)**

Following are four key areas of "applied MI efforts" that have concerned me over the years and that have been the focus of my work with MI. My concern in each area is that we act on what we know from the research—contemporary brain-mind research, the cognitive sciences, and the research on multiple intelligences. While, as Gardner points out, there are no set rules for applying the research to education, I suggest some practical restructuring implications of the research from my own perspective.

I am the first to point out, as I have elsewhere in this book, that MI is not a quick fix, nor will it provide answers to every problem or challenge we face in our schools. However, I do believe that MI brings some very important pieces to the larger educational restructuring puzzle. It is this contribution to which I turn in this final chapter.

# Multiple Intelligences
## Some Restructuring Implications

**Learning Process**

teaching **ABOUT** multiple intelligences

**Instructional Practice**

teaching **WITH** multiple intelligences

**Authentic Assessment**

assessing abilities and academics **THROUGH** multiple intelligences

**Curriculum Design**

teaching **FOR** multiple intelligences

# Restructuring Instructional Practice

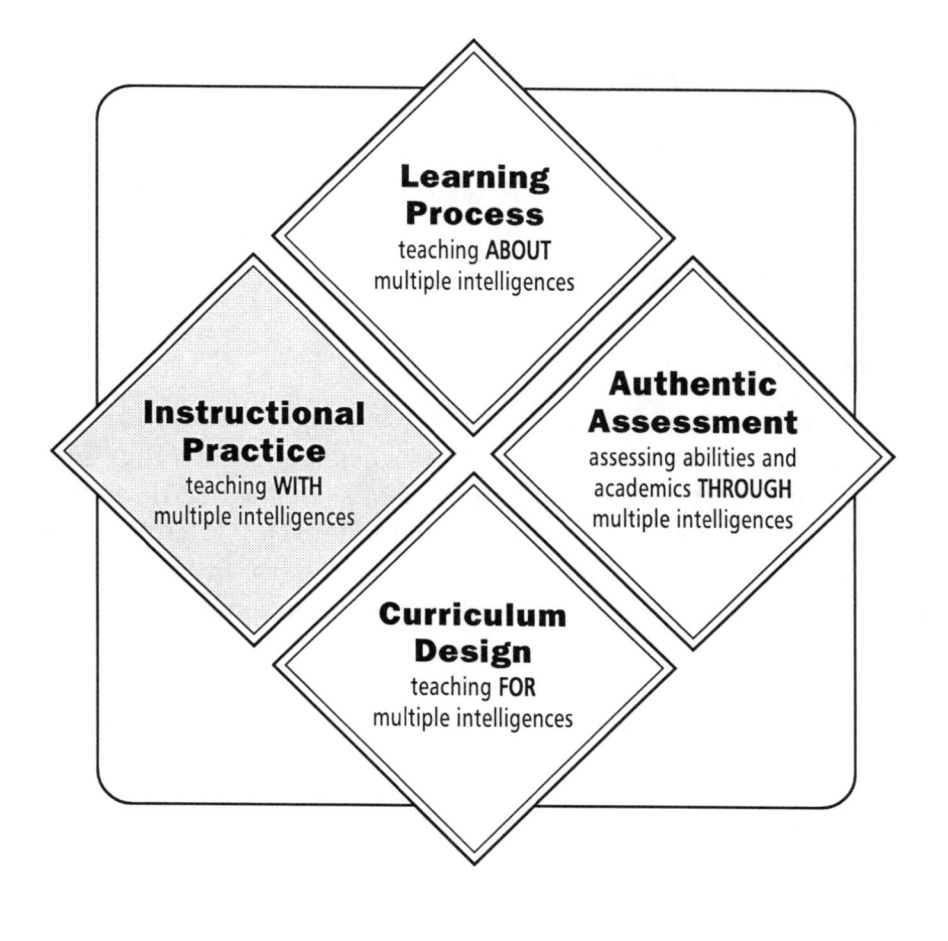

**Learning Process**
teaching ABOUT
multiple intelligences

**Instructional Practice**
teaching WITH
multiple intelligences

**Authentic Assessment**
assessing abilities and
academics THROUGH
multiple intelligences

**Curriculum Design**
teaching FOR
multiple intelligences

## Teaching *with* Multiple Intelligences

### Research Finding

*The various intelligences can be awakened or triggered in the brain-mind-body system, and once awakened, they can be amplified, enhanced, and expanded.* The eight identified intelligences are part of our neurology and physiology as human beings; however, they tend to develop differently given various environmental, cultural, and genetic influences. Nevertheless, given the plasticity of the human brain, each intelligence can be strengthened and its "knowing capacities" vastly expanded.

## Restructuring Implications

■ *We should employ intelligence-specific exercises, games, puzzles, and activities* to help students make the neurological shift into the various modalities of knowing, especially when conducting lessons that emphasize or focus on a single intelligence.

■ *The various media and tools for stimulating the different intelligences must be abundantly present in the classroom,* and we must encourage students and teach them how to use the tools to gain knowledge, process information from a lesson, know and learn, and create a range of products that demonstrate their understanding.

## Research Finding

*Each intelligence has its own distinct language, vernacular, jargon, and modus operandi.* In other words, each intelligence has a unique symbol system. The symbol systems are manifested in a variety of precise notational forms that include such things as written words, artistic forms, numbers, musical notes, dance steps, body language, visual internal and external symbols, and human-relating or group-processing methods. The modus operandi involves a series of specific intelligence-compatible processes, methodologies, techniques, strategies, and modalities.

## Restructuring Implications

■ *We must couch multiple intelligence lessons in the unique language and symbol systems of the various intelligences,* which include, but go beyond the traditional "reading, writing, and 'rithmetic" biases of the existing curriculum; students must learn how to "speak the language" of each intelligence and to interpret the symbols each employs.

■ *We should stage lessons so that they are intelligence compatible, that is, in line with the operating mode of each intelligence.* We should use intelligence-awakening exercises, games, puzzles at the beginning of a lesson to stimulate, activate, or trigger a particular focus intelligence. We should design the ensuing teaching and learning with the idea of employing the specific tools, techniques, and capacities of the intelligence to help students acquire the targeted knowledge, process information, and so on.

## Research Finding

*The more levels of the brain-mind-body system that are engaged in a given situation, the greater the learning potential of that situation.* Increased neurological activity likewise increases the potential connections the brain can make with total life experience, past, present and future. Instruction should involve enough complex teaching and learning tasks that students' brains are put into highly activated states. Approximately 95 percent of current school curricula (including both teacher and student materials) comes prepackaged, so to speak, in a verbal-linguistic or logical-mathematical mode.

## Restructuring Implications

- *Daily lessons should be multisensory learning experiences* that provide students with chances to touch, see, hear, taste, dance, smell, write, discuss, draw, sculpt, paint, reflect, and sing about what they are learning. Such experiences not only create more learning connections in the brain, but also store learning in the brain's long-term memory system.

- *We should encourage students to use the full spectrum of their intelligences regularly* to acquire knowledge and to process information, as well as to deepen, amplify, and enhance their understanding.

- *We should create instructional tracking plans to ensure that we are teaching in intelligence-balanced ways,* since most teachers tend to teach in the way they were taught; it is important to reflect on the fact that one's own most comfortable and accustomed ways of teaching may be blocking some students from learning!

# Restructuring
# the Learning Process

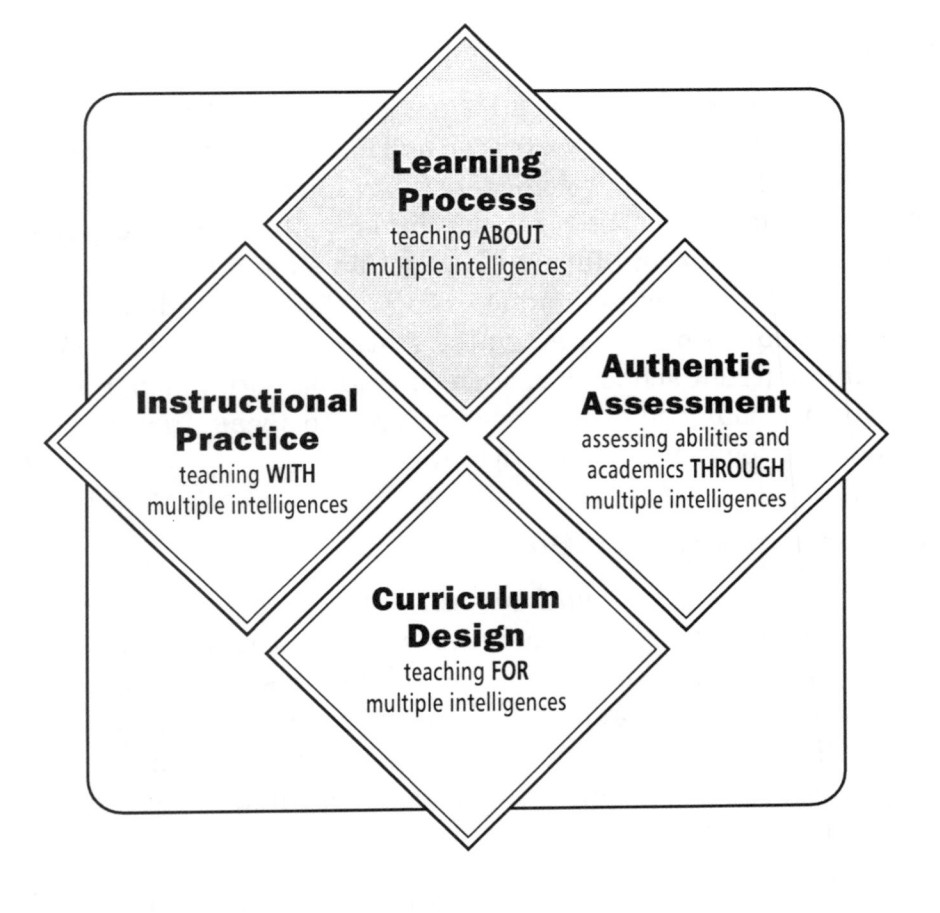

## Teaching *about* Multiple Intelligences

### Research Finding

*Intellectual capacity development follows a path from tacit to aware to strategic to reflective levels of both awareness and integration.* The tacit level involves the simple recognition of various cognitive capacities that are part of everyday life. The aware level involves a self-conscious use of the various cognitive capacities and an awareness of strengths and weaknesses. The strategic level involves the ability to use various cognitive capacities intentionally to improve problem-solving ability and to enhance personal creativity. The reflective level involves the regular integration of a range of cognitive capacities as part of one's repertoire for living.

## Restructuring Implications

■ *We should conduct community awareness programs* to help parents, school board members, community leaders, and the general public understand the theory of multiple intelligences and to show ways it can provide guidelines for contemporary school restructuring and reform efforts.

■ *We should regularly offer parent inservices on the theory of multiple intelligences.* Parents can do many things at home to nurture, encourage, even evoke the intelligences in their children. Parents know that their children are smart, even if not in the way school has traditionally valued. Likewise, these inservices can help them understand new efforts the school is making to address all the intelligences.

■ *We should teach students about multiple intelligences so they get to know themselves intellectually.* This process involves teaching them to recognize the various intelligences, making them aware of their own strong and less developed intelligence areas, and showing them how to stretch themselves to use all ways of knowing in their formal schooling and in the course of daily living.

# Restructuring Curriculum Design

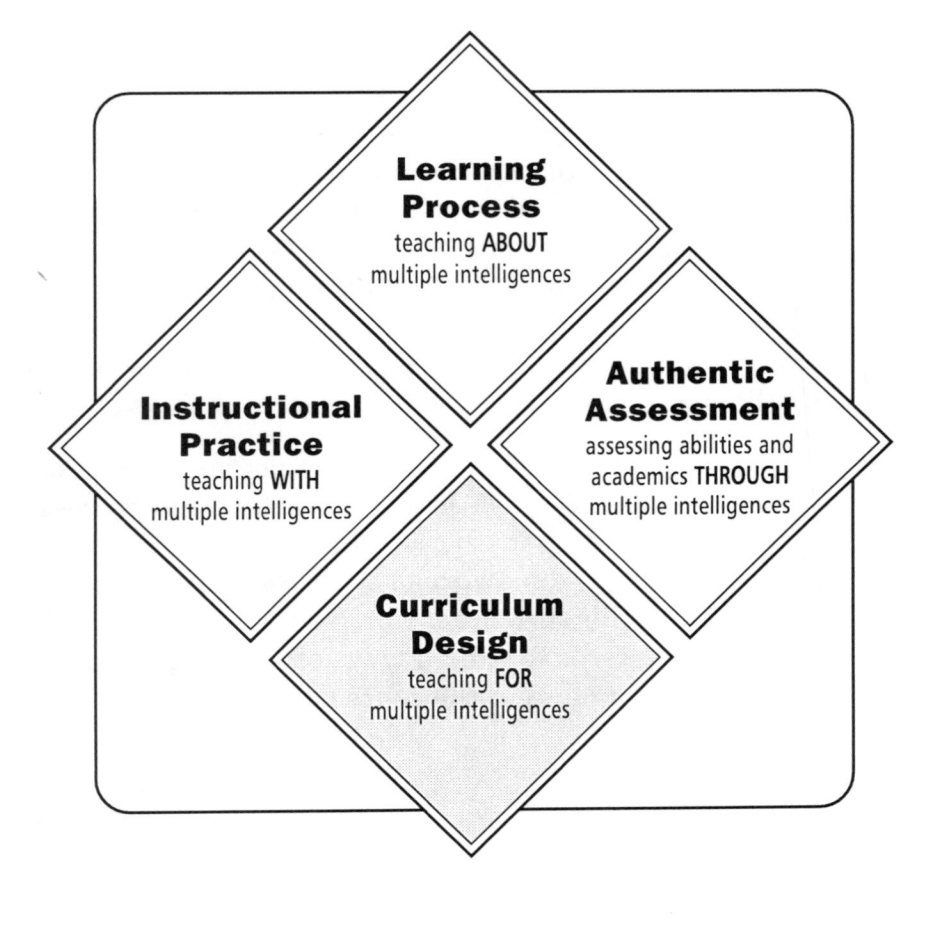

## Teaching *for* Multiple Intelligences

### Research Finding

*Each intelligence contains a core set of neurological operations or capacities that are involved in its full functioning.* These capacities can be learned, enhanced, expanded, amplified, and strengthened. If we want students to realize their full intellectual potential, we must integrate activities that systematically develop the capacities of each intelligence in and through the academic curriculum, and we must change the bias of current curriculum that values almost exclusively verbal-linguistic or logical-mathematical intelligence.

## Restructuring Implications

■ *We should integrate the various intelligence capacities into the design of curriculum units* so that students have ample opportunities to practice using them to gain knowledge, process information, and deepen their understanding.

■ *We should expand the physical education and fine arts in the curriculum (including music, art, dance, drama, poetry, storytelling, and creative writing) and incorporate them into the traditional academic areas* to help all students develop the full spectrum of their intellectual capacities; these dimensions of the curriculum should not be optional nor viewed as *extra*curricular.

■ *We should write curriculum guides in ways that value the development of the full range of intellectual capabilities, and we should hold teachers accountable for developing students' capacities in each of the eight intelligence areas,* much as we currently do with the verbal-linguistic (language arts) and logical-mathematical (math and science) parts of the curriculum.

# Restructuring Assessment

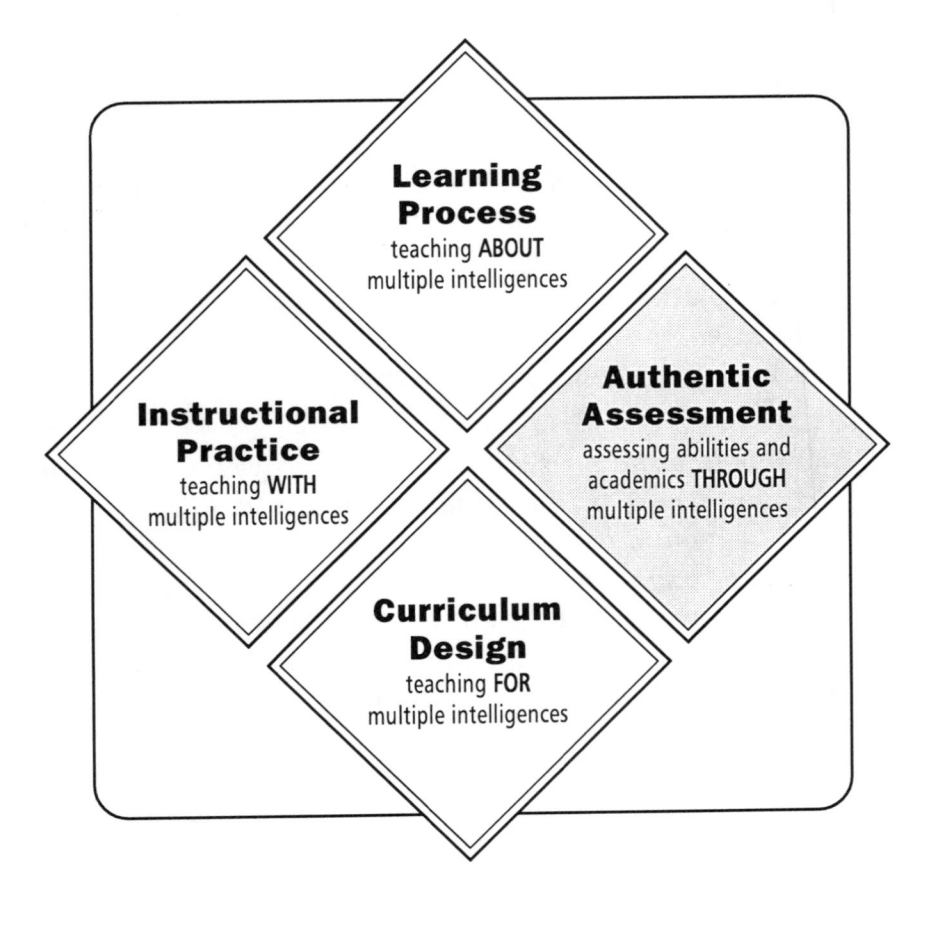

**Learning Process**
teaching ABOUT
multiple intelligences

**Instructional Practice**
teaching WITH
multiple intelligences

**Authentic Assessment**
assessing abilities and
academics THROUGH
multiple intelligences

**Curriculum Design**
teaching FOR
multiple intelligences

## Assessing Intellectual Abilities and Academic Progress *through* Multiple Intelligences

### Research Finding

*Each intelligence has its own unique developmental trajectory and taxonomy.* The intelligences tend to move through various developmental stages: from acquisition and patterning of basic skills, usually in infancy and early childhood, to the development of a more complex repertoire of skills, generally in the elementary years, to the ability to use the intelligences in a more coherent and integrated way as part of one's repertoire for living, usually in the secondary years, to the level of mastery often evident in one's vocational and avocational pursuits.

## Restructuring Implications

■ *We should expand diagnostic evaluations of students' intelligence to include all the intelligences. Such evaluations should include in-context observations of students' performing meaningful, real-life activities and tasks.* We must not limit evaluations to standard IQ or ability testing that occurs in a decontextualized, paper-and-pencil biased setting.

■ *We should make the goal of all intelligence or ability testing the creation of student intelligence profiles rather than the labeling of students.* Intelligence profiles provide a whole picture of the various factors (strengths and weaknesses, likes and dislikes) that are part of the intellectual functioning and capabilities of students.

■ *We should use these intelligence profiles as the basis for designing individualized, developmentally appropriate learning plans* and capacity-development opportunities that fully utilize students' strengths to work on developing capacity in their weaker areas.

## Research Finding

*The human brain possesses two parallel processing systems: an analytic, reflective system to explore the more objective, factual elements of a situation; and a conceptual, reflexive system that identifies the dangerous and opportunistic elements in a situation.* When our emotional-attentional systems report a problem, our first line of either defense or attack tends to be *reflexive.* Our slower *reflective,* problem-solving system is simultaneously altered, and it can affect or even override our reflexive system's response if it can come up with a better solution, or it can at least soften the response.

## Restructuring Implications

■ *We should design the school environment, curriculum, and assessment to enhance the learning process by reducing the specter of threat* when it doesn't enhance the learning process.

■ *We should blur the lines between assessment and the curriculum* because assessment is part of the regular teaching and learning process—assessment is always going on. Students won't know when they are being assessed, and more important, won't worry about it. There are no special assessment times to fear because assessment becomes a very natural part of learning.

■ *We should make intelligence-fair assessment practices the norm of district testing* because they provide an authentic means of assessing students' understanding of the curriculum. We must couch these assessment in the unique language and symbol systems of the various intelligences, and we must value them equally with a student's ability to demonstrate understanding in the verbal-linguistic or logical-mathematical modes.

■ We should make portfolios, processfolios, and intelligence domain projects, exhibits, and performances an integral part of the regular, ongoing assessment of students' progress; *they accurately and fairly document the learning journey and achievements of students, as well as their ability to transfer learning to real life.*

So what would an MI school look like? There is obviously no single, and definitely no right, answer. Or maybe the right answer is that there are multiple answers to the question, all of which flow from the wonderful multiplicity and diversity represented by the human family. The truth is there probably is no such thing as an MI school. It's probably more helpful to ask what qualities and values one should expect to find in some form in a school, district, or school division espousing a basis in MI theory. I conclude with a final quotation from Howard Gardner (1995), who says it better than I ever could:

When I visit an "MI school," I look for signs of personalization: evidence that all involved in the educational encounter take . . . differences among human beings seriously; evidence that they construct curricula, pedagogy, and assessment insofar as possible in light of these differences. All the MI posters, indeed all the references to me personally, prove to be of little avail if the youngsters continue to be treated in homogenized fashion. By the same token, whether or not members of the staff have even heard of MI theory, I would be happy to send my children to a school with the following characteristics: differences among youngsters are taken seriously, knowledge about differences is shared with children and parents, children gradually assume responsibility for their own learning, and materials that are worth knowing are presented in ways that afford each child the maximum opportunity to master those materials and to show others (and themselves) what they have learned and understood. (208)

I believe, and have witnessed firsthand, that an MI approach to teaching and learning creates this possibility for all involved in the journey, teachers and students alike, for it evokes all that we can be as human beings!

# Bibliography

Armstrong, T. 1987. *In Their Own Way: Discovering and Encouraging Your Child's Personal Learning Style.* Los Angeles: J. P. Tarcher.

———. 1993. *Seven Kinds of Smart: Identifying and Developing Your Many Intelligences.* New York: Penguin.

Bellanca, J., and R. Fogarty. 1989. *Patterns for Thinking, Patterns for Transfer.* Palatine, Ill.: Skylight.

Beyer, B. 1987. *Practical Strategies for the Teaching of Thinking.* Boston: Allyn and Bacon.

Blair, J., and R. N. Caine, eds. 1995. *Integrative Learning as the Pathway to Teaching Holism, Complexity, and Interconnectedness.* Lewiston, N.Y.: Edwin Mellen Press.

Bloom, A. 1987. *The Closing of the American Mind.* New York: Simon and Schuster.

Bloom, B. J. 1984. *Taxonomy of Educational Objectives: The Classification of Educational Goals.* New York: Longman.

Bolanos, P. J. 1990. "Restructuring the Curriculum." *Principal* 69, 3: 13–14.

Brophy, J. 1998. *Motivating Students to Learn.* Boston: McGraw-Hill.

Bruner, J. 1975. *Toward a Theory of Instruction.* Cambridge, Mass.: Belkamp Press.

Caine, R. N., and G. Caine. 1997. *Education on the Edge of Possibility.* Alexandria, Va.: ASCD.

———. 1994a. *Making Connections: Teaching and the Human Brain.* Rev. ed. Alexandria, Va.: ASCD.

———. 1990. "Understanding a Brain-Based Approach to Learning and Teaching." *Educational Leadership* 48, 2: 66–70.

Campbell, B. 1994. *The Multiple Intelligences Handbook: Lesson Plans and More.* Stanwood, Wash.: Stanwood.

Campbell, L., B. Campbell, and D. Dickinson. 1992. *Teaching and Learning through Multiple Intelligences.* Seattle, Wash.: New Horizons or Learning.

Chapman, C. 1993. *If the Shoe Fits . . . How to Develop Multiple Intelligences in the Classroom.* Palatine, Ill.: Skylight.

Clark Jr., E. 1992. "The Search for a New Educational Paradigm." *If Minds Matter: A Foreword to the Future,* vol. 1. Palatine, Ill.: Skylight. 25–40.

Costa, A. 1991a. *Developing Minds.* Rev. ed. Alexandra, Va.: ASCD.

———. 1984. "Mediating the Metacognitive." *Educational Leadership* 42, 3: 57–62.

———. 1991b. *The School as a Home for the Mind.* Palatine, Ill.: Skylight.

———. 1981. "Teaching for Intelligent Behavior." *Educational Leadership* 39, 1: 29–31.

Csikszentmihalyi, M. 1991. *Flow: The Psychology of Optimal Experience.* New York: Harper.

Darling-Hammond, L. 1997. *The Right to Learn.* San Francisco: Jossey-Bass.

de Bono, E. 1992. *Serious Creativity: Using the Power of Lateral Thinking to Create New Ideas.* New York: HarperCollins.

Diamond, M. C., and J. Hopson. 1998. *Magic Trees of the Mind: How to Nurture Your Child's Intelligence, Creativity, and Healthy Emotions from Birth through Adolescence.* New York: Dutton.

Dickinson, D. 1987. *New Developments in Cognitive Research.* Seattle, Wash.: New Horizons for Learning.

———. 1992. "Technology and the Multiple Intelligences." *Intelligence Connections* 1: 2–3.

Dickinson, D., ed. 1991. *Creating the Future: Perspectives on Educational Change.* Aston Clinton, Bucks, U.K.: Accelerated Learning Systems.

Diez, M. E., and C. J. Moon. 1992. "What Do We Want Students to Know? . . . and Other Important Questions." *Educational Leadership* 49, 8: 38–41.

Educational Testing Service and Harvard Project Zero. 1991. *Arts Propel: An Introductory Handbook.* Cambridge, Mass.: Harvard Graduate School of Education.

Eisner, E. 1993. "Why Standards May not Improve Schools." *Educational Leadership* 50, 5: 76–77.

Feuerstein, R. 1980. *Instrumental Enrichment: An Intervention Program for Cognitive Modifiability.* Baltimore, Md.: University Park Press.

Fulghum, R. 1988. *All I Really Need to Know I Learned in Kindergarten.* New York: Random House.

Fogarty, R. 1991. *The Mindful School: How to Integrate the Curricula.* Palatine, Ill.: Skylight.

Gardner, Howard. 1996. "Are There Additional Intelligences?" Available through Harvard Graduate School of Education, Cambridge, Mass.

———. 1987. "Developing the Spectrum of Human Intelligences: Teaching in the Eighties: A Need to Change." *Harvard Educational Review* 57: 87–93.

———. 1982. *Developmental Psychology: An Introduction.* Boston: Little, Brown.

———. 1999. *The Disciplined Mind: What All Students Should Understand.* New York: Simon and Schuster.

———. 1983. *Frames of Mind: The Theory of Multiple Intelligences.* New York: Basic.

———. 1993. *Multiple Intelligences: The Theory in Practice.* New York: Basic.

———. 1995. "Reflections on Multiple Intelligences: Myths and Messages." *Phi Delta Kappan* 77, 3: 200–203, 206–9.

———. 1991. *The Unschooled Mind: How Children Think and How Schools Should Teach.* New York: Basic.

Glasser, W. 1986. *Control Theory in the Classroom.* New York: Perennial Library.

Glatthom, A. A. 1994. *Developing a Quality Curriculum*. Alexandria, Va.: ASCD.

Glickman, C. 1991. "Pretending Not to Know What We Know." *Educational Leadership* 48, 8: 4–9.

Goleman, D. 1995. *Emotional Intelligence*. New York: Bantam.

Gorman, B., and W. Johnson. 1991. *Successful Schooling for Everyone*. Bloomington, Ind.: National Educational Services.

Gould, S. 1981. *The Mismeasure of Man*. New York: Norton.

Gregorc, A. 1982. *A Style Delineator*. Maynard, Mass.: Gabriel Systems.

Guilford, J. P. 1967. *The Nature of Human Intelligence*. New York: McGraw-Hill.

Haggerty, B. 1995. *Nurturing Intelligences: A Guide to Multiple Intelligence Theory and Practice*. New York: Addison Wesley.

Hansen, J. M., and J. Childs. 1998. "Creating a School Where People Like to Be." *Educational Leadership* 56, 1: 14–17.

Harman, W. 1988. *The Global Mind Change: The Promise of the Last Years of the Twentieth Century*. Indianapolis, Ind.: Knowledge Systems.

Harman, W., and H. Rheingold. 1985. *Higher Creativity: Liberating the Unconscious for Breakthrough Insights*. Los Angeles: J. P. Tarcher.

Harris, P. 1992. "Restructuring for Learning." *If Minds Matter: A Foreword to the Future,* vol. 1. Palatine, Ill.: Skylight.

Hart, L. 1983. *Human Brain and Human Learning*. Village of Oak Creek, Ariz.: Books for Educators.

Hoerr, T. forthcoming. *Becoming an MI School: Using Multiple Intelligences for Student and Teacher Success*. Alexandria, Va.: ASCD

Houston, J. 1980. *Lifeforce: The Psycho-Historical Recovery of the Self*. New York: Delacorte Press.

———. 1982. *The Possible Human: A Course in Extending Your Physical, Mental, and Creative Abilities*. Los Angeles: J. P. Tarcher.

Jacobs, H. H. 1990. *Interdisciplinary Curriculum: Design and Implementation.* Alexandria, Va.: ASCD.

Jacobs, H. H., and J. H. Borland. 1986. "The Interdisciplinary Concept Model: Theory and Practice." *Gifted Child Quarterly* 30, 4: 159–63.

Jensen, E. 1998. *Teaching with the Brain in Mind.* Alexandria, Va.: ASCD.

Kagan, S., and M. Kagan. 1998. *Multiple Intelligences: The Complete MI Book.* San Clemente, Calif.: Kagan Cooperative Learning.

Kalick, B. 1989. *Changing Schools into Communities for Thinking.* Grand Forks, N.D.: University of North Dakota Press.

Kohn, A. 1996. *Beyond Discipline: From Compliance to Community.* Alexandria, Va.: ASCD.

Kovalik, S. 1993. *Integrated Thematic Instruction: The Model.* Village of Oak Creek, Ariz.: Susan Kovalik and Associates.

Krechevsky, M. 1991. "Project Spectrum: An Innovative Assessment Alternative." *Educational Leadership* 48, 5: 43–48.

Krechevsky, M., T. Hoerr, and H. Gardner. 1995. "Complementary Energies: Implementing MI Theory from the Lab and from the Field." In *Creating New Educational Communities: Schools and Classrooms Where All Children Can Be Smart.* Ed. Jeannie Oakes and Karen H. Quartz. Chicago: University of Chicago Press, 166–86.

Lazear, David. 1999. *Pathways of Learning: Teaching Students and Parents about Multiple Intelligences.* Tucson, Ariz.: Zephyr Press.

———. 1998a. *Eight Ways of Knowing: Teaching for Multiple Intelligences.* Arlington Heights, Ill.: Skylight.

———. 1998b. *Eight Ways of Teaching: The Artistry of Teaching with Multiple Intelligences.* Arlington Heights, Ill.: Skylight.

———. 1998c. *Multiple Intelligence Approaches to Assessment: Solving the Assessment Conundrum.* Rev. ed. Tucson, Ariz.: Zephyr Press.

———. 1989. "Multiple Intelligences and How We Nurture Them." *Cogitore* 4, 1: 1, 4–5.

———. 1998d. *The Rubrics Way: Using MI to Assess Understanding.* Tucson, Ariz.: Zephyr Press.

New City School Faculty. 1994. *Celebrating Multiple Intelligences: Teaching for Success.* St. Louis, Mo.: New City School.

———. 1996. *Succeeding with Multiple Intelligences: Teaching through the Personal Intelligences.* St. Louis, Mo.: New City School.

Orlich, D. 1994. *Teaching Strategies.* Lexington, Mass. D. C. Heath.

Perkins, D. 1995. *Outsmarting IQ: The Emerging Science of Learnable Intelligence.* New York: Free Press.

———. 1992. *Smart Schools: From Training Memories to Educating Minds.* New York: Free Press.

Perkins, D., and G. Solomon. 1988. "Teaching for Transfer." *Educational Leadership* 46, 1: 22–32.

Piaget, J. 1972. *The Psychology of Intelligence.* Totowa, N.J.: Littlefield Adams.

Piaget, J., and B. Inhelder. 1972. *Psychology of the Child.* Tr. Helen Weaver. New York: Basic.

Resnick, L. B., and Klopfer, L. 1989. *Toward the Thinking Curriculum: Current Cognitive Research.* Alexandria, Va.: ASCD.

Russell, P. 1995. *The Global Brain Awakens: Our Next Evolutionary Leap.* Palo Alto, Calif.: Global Brain.

Schlechty, P. 1990. *Schools for the 21st Century.* San Francisco: Jossey-Bass.

Sizer, T. R., and B. Rogers. 1993. "Designing Standards: Achieving the Delicate Balance." *Educational Leadership* 50, 5: 24–26.

Smith, F. 1986. *Insult to Intelligences: The Bureaucratic Invasion of Our Classrooms.* Portsmouth, N.H.: Heinemann Educational.

Sternberg, R. 1984. *Beyond I.Q.: A Triarchic Theory of Human Intelligence.* New York: Cambridge University Press.

———. 1984. "How Can We Teach Intelligence?" *Educational Leadership* 42, 1: 38–48.

————. 1986. *Intelligence Applied: Understanding and Increasing Your Intellectual Skills.* San Diego: Harcourt Brace Jovanovich.

————. 1991. "Thinking Styles: Keys to Understanding Student Performance." *Inquiry: Critical Thinking across the Disciplines* 7, 3: 1, 32–38.

Stiggins, R., E. Rubel, and E. Quellmalz. 1986. *Measuring Thinking Skills in the Classroom: A Teacher's Guide.* Portland, Ore.: Northwest Regional Laboratory.

Ulrey, D., and J. Ulrey. 1992. "Developmentally Appropriate Practices Meet Multiple Intelligences." *Intelligence Connections* 2, 1: 4–6.

Wahl, Mark. 1997. *Math for Humans: Teaching Math through 7 Intelligences.* Langley, Wash.: LivnLern Press.

Wiggins, G. 1991. "Standards, Not Standardization: Evoking Quality Student Work." *Educational Leadership* 48, 4: 18–25.

# More Practical MI Resources from *Zephyr Press!*

## THE MI STRATEGY BANK
*by Ellen Arnold, Ed.D.*
Grades K–12

Do you often ask yourself, "How can I best teach this learner?" With *The MI Strategy Bank*, you'll find the answer easier than ever before! You'll quickly recognize how your students learn best and have precise methods to instruct them more effectively. Discover a great tool for designing and implementing plans for all different kinds of learners.

For each intelligence you'll have lists of ready-to-use strategies to improve—
- Learning
- Reading
- Note-taking
- Writing
- Spelling
- Math facts

**1099-W . . . $16**

## SCIENCE THROUGH MULTIPLE INTELLIGENCES
*Patterns That Inspire Inquiry*
by Robert Barkman, Ph.D.
Grades 1–12

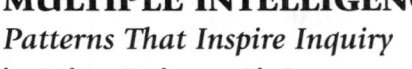

All students can learn science if they are allowed to use their multiple intelligences to interpret their environment. Each activity in *Science through Multiple Intelligences* is built upon an ecological principle, scientific objective, and a national science standard. With each of the 36 outdoor lessons, you'll also have tasks, concepts, resources, and enrichment questions. Students construct knowledge from patterns they discover in lessons ranging from squirrels to leaves.

You'll have—
- Ways to develop the key scientific skill of pattern recognition
- A brain-compatible discovery/inquiry method of teaching science
- New tools to reach your learner such as visual-spatial, musical, or bodily-kinesthetic observation

**1093-W . . . $ 39**

## DISCOVERING THE NATURALIST INTELLIGENCE
*Science in the School Yard*
by Jenna Glock, M.Ed., Susan Wertz, M.A., and Maggie Meyer, M.A.
foreword by Thomas R. Hoerr, Ph.D.
Grades 1–6

By popular demand, here is the tool you need to help you—
- Define what the naturalist intelligence is and can achieve
- Identify naturalist traits in your students with an observational checklist
- Meet national science standards while using MI techniques in every lesson
- Strengthen your students' use of the naturalist intelligence with more than 30 outdoor lessons

Each lesson includes—
- List of intelligences used
- Literature entry point
- Curriculum extensions
- Assessments that check for understanding
- Reflection prompts for journals
- Tightly formatted directions for teachers

**1095-W . . . $29**

## SQUARE PEGS
*Building Success in School and Life through MI*
by Jean Bowen, Carol King, M.Ed., and Marianne Hawkins, M.Ed.
Grades 4–12

Teach your students learning skills they'll use throughout life. An MI book that goes beyond the classroom! You'll find this resource set up in an easy-to-use format. Each activity has clear objectives—no second-guessing or confusion.

With numerous reproducible activity sheets, teacher resource sheets, wall posters, and cartoons, your students learn how to—
- Take control of their attitudes, thoughts, and feelings
- Use the personal intelligences to create a positive learning environment for themselves
- Develop strategies for applying each type of intelligence to a variety of curricular areas
- Develop general life skills (focus, organization, communication)

**1079-W . . . $36**

P.O. Box 66006, Tucson, AZ 85728-6006 ◆ Telephone 800-232-2187 ◆ FAX 520-323-9402 ◆ http://www.zephyrpress.com

## Now Includes the Naturalist
### PATHWAYS OF LEARNING
*Teaching Students and Parents about Multiple Intelligences*

by David Lazear;
foreword by Arthur Costa
*Grades K–12+*

You'll find 20 reproducible activities, 120 lesson extensions, personal reflection logs, and activities to involve parents. Each step encompasses a wider spiral of understanding.

**1045-W . . . $37**

### MI IN ACTION
*Your School and the Multiple Intelligences*

in collaboration with David Lazear
*Staff Development*

Put these information-packed videos to work for you! You'll be introduced to MI by leading experts. You'll get these 5 videos—an overview, teaching MI in the elementary grades, MI in middle and high school, MI assessment, and an MI guide for parents.

*Five 20-minute, full-color, VHS videotapes, and five 8–10 page accompanying booklets.*

**1705-W . . . $245**

### TAP YOUR MULTIPLE INTELLIGENCES
*Posters for the Classroom*

text by David Lazear
illustrations by Nancy Margulies
*Grades 3–12*

This handy set of 8 colorful posters will remind your students to use all of their intelligences. Includes the naturalist!

*8 full-color, 11" x 17" posters.*
**1811-W . . . $27**

## Shop online for more products and great specials at http://zephyrpress.com

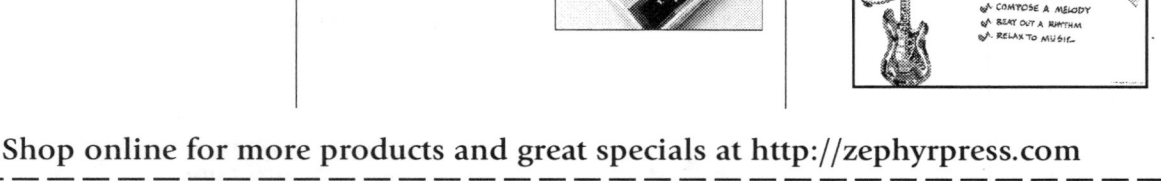

| Qty. | Item # | Title | Unit Price | Total |
|------|--------|-------|-----------|-------|
|      |        |       |           |       |
|      |        |       |           |       |
|      |        |       |           |       |
|      |        |       |           |       |
|      |        |       |           |       |
|      |        |       |           |       |
|      |        |       |           |       |
|      |        | Subtotal |        |       |
|      |        | Sales Tax (AZ residents, 5%) | | |
|      |        | S & H (10% of subtotal, min. $4.00) | | |
|      |        | Total (U.S.funds only) | | |

Name _____

Address _____

City _____

State _____ Zip _____

Phone (_____) _____

email _____

**Method of payment (check one):**

❑ Check or Money Order ❑ Visa

❑ MasterCard ❑ Purchase Order Attached

Credit Card No. _____

Expires _____

Signature _____

CANADA: add 22% for S & H and G.S.T.

☎ **ORDER TODAY!**

Please include your phone number in case we have questions about your order.

➤ **To order write or call:**

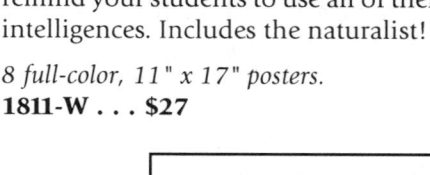

Zephyr Press®

REACHING THEIR HIGHEST POTENTIAL

P.O. Box 66006-W
Tucson, AZ 85728-6006

(800) 232-2187
(520) 322-5090
FAX (520) 323-9402